# Happy Brain Habits

Discover Over 7 Highly Effective Atomic High-Performance Habits and Achieve Success in Life and Business, Overcome Procrastination and Become Extraordinary

## Stephen Patterson

© Copyright 2019 - All rights reserved.

The content contained within this book may not be reproduced, duplicated or transmitted without direct written permission from the author or the publisher.

Under no circumstances will any blame or legal responsibility be held against the publisher, or author, for any damages, reparation, or monetary loss due to the information contained within this book. Either directly or indirectly.

**Legal Notice:**
This book is copyright protected. This book is only for personal use. You cannot amend, distribute, sell, use, quote or paraphrase any part, or the content within this book, without the consent of the author or publisher.

**Disclaimer Notice:**

Please note the information contained within this document is for educational and entertainment purposes only. All effort has been executed to present accurate, up to date, and reliable, complete information. No warranties of any kind are declared or implied. Readers acknowledge that the author is not engaging in the rendering of legal, financial, medical or professional advice. The content within this book has been derived from various sources. Please consult a licensed professional before attempting any techniques outlined in this book.

By reading this document, the reader agrees that under no circumstances is the author responsible for any losses, direct or indirect, which are incurred as a result of the use of information contained within this document, including, but not limited to, — errors, omissions, or inaccuracies.

# Contents

**Cure for the Procrastination Puzzle** _____ 1

Chapter 1:
What is Procrastination _____ 3

Chapter 2:
The Life Impact of Procrastination _____ 11

Chapter 3:
Reasons We Procrastinate _____ 19

Chapter 4:
What Can Happen with Productivity _____ 35

Chapter 5:
The Importance of Motivation _____ 43

Chapter 6:
The Impact of Willpower and Self-Discipline _____ 53

Chapter 7:
Overcoming Procrastination _____ 61

Chapter 8:
Figure Out the Reason for Your Procrastination _____ 65

**Chapter 9:**
Audit Your Goals Weekly _____ 69

**Chapter 10:**
Get Rid of Negative Self-Talk _____ 77

**Chapter 11:**
Focus on a Single Task _____ 81

**Chapter 12:**
Time Chunking _____ 89

**Chapter 13:**
Reduce Environmental Distractions _____ 97

**Chapter 14:**
Avoid Being Bored _____ 107

**Chapter 15:**
Find an Accountability Partner _____ 113

**Chapter 16:**
Leverage Your Peak-Energy _____ 117

**Chapter 17:**
Parkinson's Law _____ 125

**Chapter 18:**
Prioritize Tasks _____ 131

Chapter 19:
Reward Yourself _____ 137

Chapter 20:
FAQs _____ 143

Conclusion _____ 147

## Successful Habits of Extraordinary People — 149

Introduction — 151

Chapter 1:
Developing Effective Habits — 153

Chapter 2:
Which Habits to Stick To — 165

Chapter 3:
The Accumulation of Habits — 179

Chapter 4:
Keystone Habits and Taking Action — 193

Chapter 5:
The Secret Habits of the Successful — 207

Chapter 6:
Keys to Financial Success — 219

Chapter 7:
Keys to Social Success — 233

Chapter 8:
The Effect of Genes on Habit Formation — 241

Chapter 9:
Stacking Habits — 251

Conclusion — 261

# HAPPY BRAIN
# HABITS

2 Manuscripts - Discover Over 7 Highly Effective Atomic High Performance Habits and Achieve Success in Life and Business, Overcome Procrastination and Become Extraordinary

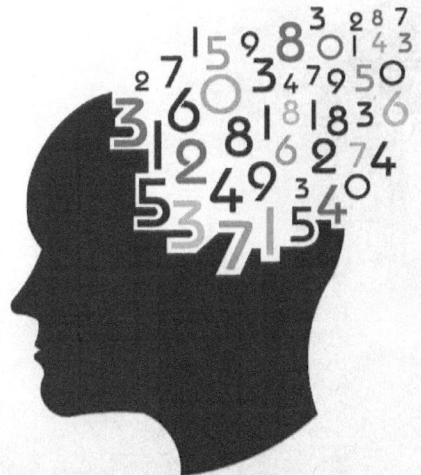

## Stephen Patterson

# Cure for the Procrastination Puzzle

Blueprint to Develop Atomic Long-Term Habits for Productivity and Get things Done - Learn Why You Do It and Master Your Time with Over 7 Highly Effective Methods

Stephen Patterson

# CURE FOR THE
# PROCRASTINATION
# PUZZLE

Blueprint to Develop Atomic Long Term Habits for Productivity and Get things Done - Learn Why You Do It and Master Your Time with Over 7 Highly Effective Methods

## Stephen Patterson

# Chapter 1:
# What is Procrastination

What exactly does procrastination mean? Pro-crustiness is a Latin word that means "belonging to tomorrow." Procrastination means "putting things off intentionally or habitually." But defining procrastination isn't that simple.

If you have ever found yourself persuading yourself to do things other than those that you should do, you have been the victim of procrastination. Most of the time, you will find yourself performing trivial tasks instead of working on important tasks.

Since the beginning of humanity, people have had to suffer from procrastination. Hesiod, the classic Greek poet, even commented on the issue in his poem *Works and Days*.

- "Do not postpone for tomorrow
- Or the day after tomorrow

- Barns are not filled by those who postpone

- And waste time in aimlessness.

- Work prospers with care;

- He who postpones wrestles with ruin."

The Roman philosopher, Seneca, even warned: "While we waste our time hesitating and postponing, life is slipping away." This quote is the main reason why it is so important that we learn how to overcome procrastination.

Procrastination is probably the main thing blocking you from living your life to its fullest. Some studies have discovered that people will often regret the things that they aren't able to accomplish than the things that they were able to do. Feelings of guilt and regret caused by missed chances will often stay with a person much longer. When a person procrastinates, they waste valuable time that could be used to do something important and meaningful. If you are able to overcome this enemy, you will notice that you can accomplish more and utilize the potential of life.

**The True Definition**

## Cure for the Procrastination Puzzle

Dr. Samuel Johnson, the author of the first comprehensive English dictionary, defined procrastination as "delay" and many still maintain that definition. The Free Dictionary defines procrastination as "slowness as a consequence of not getting around to it."

However, if all that procrastination means is to delay, then we ought to find with placing it alongside concepts like prioritizing and scheduling, but we don't. Take these two examples:

Imagine yourself as a surgeon and you are getting ready to put your patient under general anesthetic. If you discover that they just ate a large meal at a buffet, you have to hold off the operation. The reason for this is that the unconscious patient could empty the contents of their stomachs into their lungs. This would cause digestive juices to dissolve things other than the food.

Now, picture that you are in the Bahamas and have some sport-fishing planned when a category five hurricane blows in. It has winds in excess of 155 miles an hour and waves that crash in at over ten stories high. You push your plans back for fishing by a couple of days.

Both of these stories use delay, but would either of these delays that drowning or dissolving be considered as dilly-dallying? Probably not. Maybe procrastination, perhaps, could mean something more.

Timothy Picryl, a procrastination researcher, explains that "all procrastination is a delay, but not all delay is procrastination." Procrastination is a specific type of delay. Unlike these types of delays, procrastination doesn't have any rationale behind it. This extremely important distinction can be seen more often now. The American Heritage Dictionary defines it as "To put off doing something, especially out of habitual carelessness or laziness."

But the Oxford English Dictionary is the one that gets the closest to the heart of the word. Their definition of procrastination is, "often with the sense of deferring through indecision, when early action would have been preferable."

That brings us to questions of, can procrastination be good? If it's by accident that you choose to delay something purposefully because you believe it would be a good thing to do, then you are not procrastinating. This means you are prioritizing or scheduling, sometimes just so that you can get that thrill of doing something at the last moment. Procrastination is when you end up feeling as if the project should have been finished earlier, but you delayed it anyway. Basically, it means you put something off even though you expect the worse.

### Cure for the Procrastination Puzzle

The thing is, the world doesn't always work out the way we want it to, and sometimes luck will be on our side and we discover that what we have been putting off didn't have to be done after all. The way we believe the world is and the way it actually has to be at odds. Otherwise, you get lucky from time to time by procrastinating. Like if you were in Vegas playing roulette. Once in a while, you will pick the right number, but most of the time it's going to land on red.

Still, the majority of people misuse procrastination to describe useful delays, when you could use many different words to describe that problem. People will misuse a lot of other words such as "irony." Whether you want to use the word procrastination correctly or not is up to you, but I will leave you with this thought.

If, on Christmas Eve, you hear the glugging of milk and the munching of cookies coming from your living room, and after some investigation, discover a jolly and chubby old elf that has spent the last 365 days waiting to deliver colorful presents, thank him for his timeliness. He might have been able to come earlier, but you should not define his choice to delay the Yuletide cheer as procrastination.

### Today's Decision Paralysis

Now that we've gotten the real definition out of the way, let's look at how it plays out in today's world. Since the world plays into procrastination's hands, learning how to overcome it is an important skill. Over the past 100 years, the average lifespan of humans has doubled. Infant mortality has become a tenth of what it was back then. Each morning, we get up in a world that has less military conflict and less violence than any other area of our history. Most importantly, thanks to the internet, almost all information is just a few clicks away.

There are very few limits on travel. You can go almost anywhere in the world at any time. Speaking another language allows people to communicate efficiently in foreign countries. That phone you have in your pocket comes with more power than the supercomputers from 20 years ago.

There are a staggering number of opportunities in the world. Modern society believes that the freer people are, the happier they will become. If that's the case, why aren't people a lot happier now than they were in the past? With all of the extra freedom to make out own decisions and perform the things we want to, we have now become confused with what should get priority, what is crucial and what isn't, and what is right and wrong. This makes us all more demotivated.

## Cure for the Procrastination Puzzle

It's important that we set our personal vision and values straight and to establish good habits. This is what can help us to work through procrastination and all of the obstacles that come along with life.

Stephen Patterson

## Chapter 2:
## The Life Impact of Procrastination

If you were to ask a group of people to raise their hands if they view themselves as a procrastinator, a lot of hands would end up going up. While there are many people that seem to be fine with being a procrastinator, others who admit they procrastinate feel ashamed to admit it. This is normal because, in our culture, procrastination is often seen as a bad word. In America, we tend to celebrate those that are able to put their nose-to-the-grindstone. Procrastination doesn't deserve a place in our economy or culture, but is it really that bad?

There is a fine line between being pressure prompted and procrastinating. Pressure prompted means that you do your best work when you have a deadline looming over your head. While you may have to procrastinate a bit to be pressure prompted, it is procrastination within safe limits. Basically, it's a condition set that is going to provide you just enough pressure to ensure that you stay at the top of your game without creating a lot of chaos, or more importantly, not affecting your team by keeping them from being able to perform their best within the given timeframe.

But what about those who aren't only pressure prompted but real procrastinators? To clear up what I mean, I'm not talking about a person that waits to write their keynote address a couple of days before they are supposed to walk on stage, but rather the person who scribbles out a couple of notes 20 minutes before their speech. If you see this person when you look in the mirror, it is time to start thinking about how this impacts your life if it is left unmanaged.

Procrastination is a problem that impacts a person's physical and mental health, as well as their performance in the workplace and at school. A study published in Psychology Bulletin in 2007, Piers Steel, a psychologist, defined procrastination as "a self-regulatory failure leading to poor performance and reduced wellbeing." He further explained that procrastination is extremely common. Around 80 to 90 percent of college students suffer from procrastination and is something that 95% of people wants to overcome. Steel believes that procrastination is on the rise because people want to receive immediate gratification that they can get through the use of information technology and social media.

While more responsibilities and age do help the majority of people keep their procrastination in check, for some, procrastination isn't an occasional or temporary problem but something that controls their lives and limits their potential.

How bad can procrastination be? Below, I will look at a few of the negative impacts that it can have on your financial, mental, and physical wellbeing.

## Mental Health:

In 2010, a study called "I'll Go to Therapy, Eventually," discovered that stress and procrastination had a connection. The study discovered that a lot of procrastination was connected to poor mental health and fewer behaviors to help mental health such as taking time to relax.

## Physical Health:

As well as the well-documented link between mental health and procrastination, there is an increasing amount of proof that procrastination can impact a person's physical health. Fuchsia M. Sirois, in a 2003 study, discovered that procrastination was "related to poorer health, treatment delay, perceived stress, and fewer wellness behaviors." While procrastination can affect a lot of health problems, Sirois and team discovered that there were some that were more impacted than others. In a study done in 2015, she concluded that procrastination is one of the many factors that can lead to cardiovascular disease and hypertension, and further concluded that the "maladaptive coping" that is associated with procrastination exasperates the symptoms that are associated with HT/CVD.

## Workplace Satisfaction, Performance, And Success

Given how negatively procrastination impacts a person's physical and mental health, it's not surprising that it would also negatively impact a person's workplace performance. Procrastinators will often earn less, spend less time at a job, and hold jobs that have lower intrinsic value. A study performed in 2016 discovered that procrastination tends to be more common for people who are unemployed, which could mean that procrastination could cause unemployment. However, procrastination isn't something that could increase a person's likelihood of leaving a job or not having one. There is at least one other study that found that "job-lock," which means not being able to freely leave a job even if you are unhappy and there is no room for growth, could also be caused by procrastination. On a similar note, procrastination could also cause bad financial decisions.

If you're still not convinced of the detrimental effects that procrastination can have on your life, the following seven effects of procrastination are more specific and relatable.

### 1. Loss of Precious Time
How much time have you lost from procrastinating? It's not easy to figure, but I'm sure you can come up with an estimate. The worst part of procrastinating is when you realize that you are two, six, or 12 years older and nothing in your life has changed. Where did the time go?

This is a horrible feeling because you can't do anything to get that time back. All you can do is live with the helpless feeling of regret. There is nothing worse than having to feel frustrated with yourself and knowing that you could have made the situation better. All you had to do was take the first step.

### 2. Opportunities Are Blown
How many opportunities have you missed out on because you didn't jump on it when you have the chance? These are moments where you really kick yourself. What you don't see is that the opportunity could have ended up being life-changing, but you missed out.

The majority of opportunities will only come around once. There are no guaranteed second chances. Opportunities are how the world gives you more, so do yourself a favor and grab hold.

### 3. Goals Aren't Met

Procrastination will often come in full force when we start to entertain the thoughts of goals, of wanting to change or achieve something new. You could have an extremely strong desire to change, but you aren't able to take those first steps towards it. This is often perplexing and confusing. You will often think to yourself, "Why is it hard to go after something that I want?" Only you know the answer.

You are going to have to explore things a little deeper. People set goals because they want to better their lives in one way or another. If this doesn't happen because of procrastination, you will destroy your odds of bettering your life.

Figure out the root cause of your procrastination if it is keeping you from reaching your goals, otherwise, you won't attain them.

### 4. Ruined Careers

The way you work has a direct effect on your results, how well you perform, and how much you achieve. Procrastination could be preventing you from reaching deadlines or achieving your monthly goals. What kind of consequence is this going to have on your career?

You could be overlooked for a promotion or you could end up losing your job. You can do your best to hide things for a while, but long-term procrastination at work will end up ruining your career.

## 5. Low Self-Esteem
This is a common vicious cycle that people will find their self in. We often procrastinate because we have low self-esteem, but procrastinating doesn't just reinforce this feeling, it makes it stronger.

You will begin to question and doubt yourself. You will often start asking yourself, "Why can't I just do it?" Low self-esteem will destroy lives in several different ways. Low self-esteem will cause you to hold yourself back, you feel less than, and it can lead to self-sabotaging acts. Procrastination will slowly destroy your confidence.

## 6. Poor Decisions
When you make decisions from a procrastination standpoint, they will almost always be poor decisions because of where your mind is. When procrastinating, you will make decisions based on criteria that wouldn't be there otherwise such as pressure to finally make a decision.

Emotions play a big part in decisions and procrastination plays a big part in how you feel. Poor decision making will have a lot of negative effects on your life, happiness, and results.

## 7. Damaged Reputation

When you are constantly saying that you are going to do something and then you don't, your reputation is going to become tarnished. Nobody is interested in empty promises.

Besides hurting your reputation, you will damage your self-confidence and self-esteem. You will also find that procrastination will become easier every time because you will no longer feel surprised. People may end up not depending on you anymore and will hold back opportunities because they may worry that you will procrastinate and they will have to clean up your mess.

These are only a few ways your life is affected by procrastination. Procrastination works like any other habit and it can be hard to kick, but it will also make you or break you.

# Chapter 3:
# Reasons We Procrastinate

Procrastination is one of the sure-fire ways to avoid success in life. Procrastinators are self-sabotaging people and they place obstacles in their own way. They will actually pick paths that harm their performance. Why would a person do something like that?

20% of people identify themselves as a procrastinator. For these people, procrastination is their life and it affects all domains of their life. Their bills aren't paid on time. They miss out on concert tickets. They don't ever cash gift certificates or checks. Their taxes are done late. They will even put off their Christmas shopping until the day before.

It's not a trivial matter, but as a culture, we don't take it seriously. It's seen as a self-regulation problem. There may be more of it in the US than anywhere else because we tend to be nice and not call people out on their "excuses." Let's take a look at the main reasons people procrastinate.

## Better Options

A lot of people will have "Too many interests to choose just one!" That fact resonates with the majority of procrastinators. Society expects us to choose one thing and stick with it. Take Mozart for example. He started his career in music at three years old and never allowed anything to interfere, even his deafness.

But what if a person is more of a Leonardo de Vinci, Benjamin Franklin, or Maya Angelo? Where would the world be if these people that they couldn't put off finishing something until tomorrow when something new and exciting presented itself? They were all likely label procrastinators but they turned out okay. That doesn't mean all procrastination is a good thing.

When it detrimentally affects a person's life, then something needs to be done about it. The point is, people will often procrastinate because of the other things that they would rather do. Who wouldn't rather go to a concert than write a boring report for work? Still, that doesn't mean you should.

## Lack of Focus

A lack of focus in your life is another common reason a person will procrastinate. A famous idiom says "the person who does not know where they are going always travels further," but for people who are predisposed to procrastinate, this doesn't mesh all that well with them.

If you notice that you often feel directionless or that you don't have a purpose in life, then you likely have a lack of focus. If you haven't created any goals, then it's almost guaranteed that you will lack focus because you don't have a target to work towards. You could feel as if you are drifting your way through your life.

Having a lack of focus will cause procrastination because it prevents you from finding your endpoint. Instead, you will end up using all of your energy in the here and now and you won't have anything to guide you toward productivity.

A lot of younger people will suffer from a lack of focus. They haven't figured out how to set any strong targets or goals, so they will fritter away most of their day. But through effective goal setting, they can overcome this procrastination and will be able to achieve more in their life.

Setting goals for everything you do is a good idea. You can set goals for business, your finances, your career, and anything you can dream you can set a goal for. Having a good goal will encourage you to take some form of action because you won't want to disappoint yourself.

## Negative Talk

The things that people will often procrastinate on are the tasks that tend to be more difficult, or they are the tasks that you view to be more difficult. If you often blame yourself when a problem comes up, then you probably don't feel like you are able to ask for help and work through those problems.

This is only going to make your problem worse. You will often tell yourself that you can't do something or that you will mess it up. This will reinforce your procrastination because you now don't have the confidence to do anything. This is a common reason for a person to procrastinate. They lack confidence in their ability to do the job successfully. They are, in fact, more than capable of being able to do it.

This often stems from perfectionism which we will talk about later. Society can sometimes make you feel as if you have to do a perfect job at every little thing you do. That means that you won't start until you feel certain that you will be able to do it perfectly. But this is the absolute worst thing that you can do.

When you take some sort of action, you will achieve an outcome. The outcome could end up being what you are looking for or it may not be. Either way, you will learn something from it and then you can make some improvements or adjustments. If you don't take any sort of action, you won't learn anything.

## Don't Know Where to Start

What if the task ends up being too difficult, complex, or unique? What if there are a lot of moving parts that makes it unclear as to where to start? This type of uncertainty is likely to keep you from wanting to start because you don't know what your first step should be.

Even if you have figured out what your first step should be, once you start looking at the whole process, you start to realize that you may have underestimated how much commitment and time it is going to take to finish the task.

How do you overcome this problem? One of the best ways is to use the "getting things done" approach. This is going to help you to break the tasks down into smaller tasks.

## No Motivation

Have you ever had the thought that life has gotten in your way, and you haven't been able to accomplish the things you were supposed to? This lack of motivation can end up coming from many different causes, which includes:

- Unclear goals
- Working in a bad environment
- Lack of confidence
- You are around a lot of negativity
- You've not been successful in the past
- Can't find new ideas
- Unexpected emergency
- Other priorities
- Stress
- Fatigue
- Lack of energy

Carnegie Melon University performed a study that found people lack motivation when they can't find value in the possible outcome of their work. But, if people can see how their work is going to connect to their concerns, interests, and goals, they are more likely to like their work and become motivated to invest their energy and time.

The National Academies of Sciences, Engineering, and Medicine published a study that said motivation was made up of two things — goal choice and self-confidence. Self-confidence doesn't give a person motivation on its own but gives a person a judgment about their capabilities for accomplishing their goal

## Low Energy

Another common reason for procrastination is low energy levels. If you lack energy, then it's probably a good guess that you won't feel like doing all that much.

This is a common problem for people who have an unhealthy lifestyle. Whether you don't get enough sleep or you eat foods that cause you to feel tired and sluggish, lifestyle facts are able to play a very big part into how inclined you are to get up and do something.

It should be fairly easy to find the problem area in your life. If you are interested in being productive and active, but you lack the actual physical energy to do something, then you probably have a problem with low energy levels.

The cure for this is to try to develop healthier lifestyles. Try to experiment with your exercise, sleep, and diet to figure out the balance that will work for you. There is a whole host of useful info that you can find online to make positive changes in your life, and you probably already have a good idea of the changes that you need to make.

If you aren't able to raise those energy levels, then you may want to speak with your healthcare provider to rule out any underlying cause of your low energy.

## Feel Overwhelmed

When you take your first look at a difficult job or a big project, it can become overwhelming to notice how much work you are going to have to do. This doesn't get helped by the fact that you will automatically assume that you will have to do everything by yourself, and you also don't take into account the amount of time that you have to get the job done.

To make sure that you don't get overwhelmed, you will want to break your job down into smaller tasks. This is going to be a common thing that you notice throughout this book. Breaking a project down into smaller parts will help a lot with procrastination.

It's important to remember when you feel overwhelmed, that you can only do so much in one day. Unless you have already delayed the project so much that you have to do it all in one day, you shouldn't be faced with that problem.

## Perfectionism

Maybe you are afraid that you are going to make a mistake in your project and then expose a weakness to those around you. The fear of making a mistake is a very real thing and it can be so bad that people will put off some of their most important projects because of it.

Carol Dweck, Ph.D., a Stanford University psychologist, talks about the power of a person's mindset. She relates a person's success in the arts, work, sports, school, and other parts of the human endeavor to the way a person thinks about their abilities and talents.

She explains that people will either have a growth mindset or a fixed mindset. Those that have a fixed mindset think that the abilities they have can't get any better, so they focus on their current talents or intelligence and believe that they can't develop them.

They honestly believe that they were born with what they have and that there isn't anything they can do to make it better. These people will also believe that they don't need effort for success if they have talent. They think that the talent is natural.

A fixed mindset can be very dangerous because it hinders a person's ability to make positive changes, grow, and learn.

Alternatively, a growth mindset will let a person believe that their abilities are able to prosper and can be developed through hard work and dedication. They believe that a person's talents and brains are just a starting point. They are born with their strengths, but they don't have a limit on what they can do. The growth mindset helps to create a desire to learn and gives them the ability to overcome their problems to be successful.

Dweck also explained that a person's mindset can reveal how great managers, teachers, and parents can advance within their careers and achieve amazing things. When you have the right mindset, a person can motivate, teach, and lead in a way that is able to positively change the lives of others.

Hillary Rettig believes that people who procrastinate because of perfectionism will often have a fixed mindset. This means that they will avoid doing things because they are worried that they will make a mistake and look less than perfect. They expect their work to be perfect.

Since they have the belief that they will fail if the task doesn't line up with their talents, it is best to avoid until it has to be done.

While some people believe that being a perfectionist is a good thing, it actually ends up being detrimental. It comes with a very dangerous mix of anti-productive attitudes and habits that discourage progress. Although it is often confused with having high standards, perfectionism limits success to something that is unrealistic. This is a standard that won't ever be achieved, so why even try?

### Fear of Success
Everybody is pretty familiar with a fear of failure, but there is another side to that coin and that's a fear of success. This is when a person procrastinates because they are afraid of the consequences of their achievements. They may fear that they will do a good job, and then next time, more will be expected from them. It could be succeeding puts them in the limelight, but they prefer to be in the background.

This type of procrastination may indicate that there is an internal identity conflict. If your achievement and self-worth are connected, then you may find that you question yourself about how much you have to do in order to be "good enough." Every success will only set you up for another, bigger challenge.

If your family acceptance and self-worth are connected, then how much more will you have to do to make them satisfied? Every success will open a door to higher expectations.

This will often lead to feelings of identity loss and you may not be able to claim your successes as your own. Procrastination or inaction may be the way that you cope with all of the pressures you are placing on yourself by trying to be "good enough."

## Fear of Failure or The Unknown

Imagine this, you wake up one morning and notice a new mole has appeared on your arm. You start to feel anxious about the fact that it could be cancer, so you avoid having it checked and hope that it will go away. Does this sound like something you would do? Sometimes people are afraid to do something because they are afraid that it is going to reveal something they don't want.

As it turns out, "What you don't know can't hurt you," isn't all that true. In nearly every single case, if you try to ignore something for too long because you hope it will go away, it is only going to get worse.

University of Michigan researchers performed a study on the effects of letting misinformation stay in a person's mind. The study found that misinformation can stay in a person's memory and continue to influence the way they think, even if they know that they were mistaken. They are also more likely to use the misinformation, especially if it fits into their existing beliefs and create a logical story. This will then cause them to spread the misinformation to others.

This study can be applied to politics, the environment, and to individuals. When you have preconceived notions or misinformation about health issues like, "cancer doesn't run in my family, so it's probably okay," or "the mole is going to go away with some time," can end up doing a lot of damage. The researchers also discovered that a person's personal views and beliefs could end up being big obstacles for changing the believed misinformation. Additionally, attempting to provide them with an unwanted truth that goes against what they had believed can backfire and increase their incorrect ideas. When it comes to personal health problems, ignoring issues instead of facing them head-on can definitely lead to severe problems or death.

Really think about this. What if that mole was cancer that could be easily treated during the early stages, but can end up becoming malignant if it's ignored? If you are proactive in getting it checked out, it would be a simple fix. Or you could decide to procrastinate because you think that everything is going to be fine. This is when what you don't know can hurt you, and your beliefs that it is going to go away on its own will end up being detrimental.

Some other good examples of this problem include not going to the dentist and continuing to believe that the cavity you think you have is going to be okay. Maybe you aren't interested in doing your taxes because until you are faced with the fact that you will have to pay, you don't have to think about it. Maybe you are avoiding a conversation with your significant other to delay the argument that it could create. Every single one of these causes for procrastination is common.

All of this connects back to what the researchers at the University of Michigan found out because in all of these cases the person is not interested in learning the truth. They feel more at ease with the possibility that all will be okay. Ignorance is bliss, so we procrastinate in order to stay happy and ignorant. However, when you ignore these problems, it can lead to grave circumstances.

Knowledge is power. Even if it turns out to be negative, you didn't get the promotion, the mole is cancer and you own the government money, you will have more opportunities to overcome an even worse situation. Knowing this information is only half of it. After that, you will have to do something to correct it if needed. The next time you think about procrastinating, ask yourself these questions:

- Am I really scared, or have I been told something scary?

- Am I looking to protect myself from a specific outcome?

- Will I be able to handle the outcome?

- Am I afraid of the result or the process?

- Am I trying to convince myself of things that aren't true?

- How often do people die from having to do this?

- What am I going to gain in the long run if I keep putting this off?

- Why am I putting this off?

- What can happen if I continue to ignore the problem?

- What is the worst thing that could happen?

- What is it that I am afraid of?

Stephen Patterson

## Chapter 4:
## What Can Happen with Productivity

Americans enjoy work. They like to do it. It's actually very common for business professionals to work more than 50 hours a week. Some information suggests that the US is one of a few countries that don't have a requirement for time off for employees.

Some cities work their employees more than others. Columbia, Missouri received the title of the hardest working city by Forbes, which was followed by Hartford, Connecticut, and then Norfolk, Virginia.

But does being productive mean, you have to be a workaholic? Why is that Americans are so obsessed about being productive and what types of factors encourage this behavior?

When you look at productivity from a business definition, it is defined as, "a measure of the efficiency of a person, machine, factory, or system in converting inputs into useful outputs." By that definition, American workers have increased their productivity for the past few years.

However, wages which these workers directly connect with the productivity have stayed the same.

Studies and experts have discovered that productivity in humans is impacted by psychological factors. And the answer is bigger than looking at pictures of cuddly little animals.

The way the brain functions plays a big role in why and how people are productive or not so productive. Several different experiments that were performed at a factory just outside of Chicago, between the years of 1924 and 1932, which was later called the Hawthorne Effect, found that the productivity of the workers was increased because of psychological stimulus that made them feel important or singled out.

According to David M. Reiss, MD, this study makes sense for the fact that the average person, because whether unconsciously or consciously will feel insecure and have some form of vulnerabilities of self-esteem, so any intervention that is able to reduce those insecurities and help their self-esteem will make the mood better, improve productivity, reduce anxiety, and improve their motivation.

If the person is singled out in such a way that makes it feel parental, people that tend to be dependent will often respond in a positive manner, whereas if a person is more narcissistic, it will be counterproductive because they feel demeaned.

Reiss also said that those who have lower self-esteem could end up feeling as if they don't deserve any attention, which will trigger anxiety or guilt that could end up being counterproductive. The average person and those with mild narcissistic tendencies will thrive with attention. Those who have a severe narcissistic personality or are antisocial will often react in a smug way and feel as if it was about time that they were recognized, which may cause resentment, a reaction to "rest on their laurels" once they receive attention, and then "ease up" instead of being motivated.

Everybody dreads to hear the term "busy work." Among Americans, the definition of busy work means projects or assignments that are used to waste time but are in no way productive or constructive. This is common in education, but it can happen just as often in the workplace.

The issue with busy work, besides the fact that employees will become frustrated and their morale will suffer is that many will confuse busy work with productivity. Even if this kind of work causes urgency, it doesn't necessarily mean that it is productive work. While productivity can help you overcome procrastination, knowing the difference between productivity and busy work is important. If you allow yourself to become burned out by busy work, you will be more likely to procrastinate on the important work. We're going to take a quick look at what are non-productive tasks like updating or reading social media, holding meetings, and checking emails. While these tasks could be important, they are endless and time-consuming.

Take this scenario for example. A person can sort through over 200 emails in less than 15 minutes if they need to, so why is that it will take hours each day for them to check half as many if they don't have to.

They come to the conclusion that by accepting an email, you allow it to be an interruption and you stop something that was productive. You are working on getting something done, almost completely finish, and *ding* an email. You look. It's from your grandma, boss, or colleague. You quit everything and respond.

All of these tiny little interruptions will mess with your focus and concentration, and if you let this happen several times during the day, it can have a large impact on your level of productivity. To be productive and not busy, you need to:

- Stay off social media.

## Cure for the Procrastination Puzzle

- Stop "staying updated" on blogs and news.

- Keep meetings short or avoid them altogether.

- Minimize the amount of time you spend on your phone.

- Check your emails only a couple of times during the day.

However, there are a lot of jobs where constantly using social media all day and perusing blogs for trends is completely normal and even expected. These types of workers and those who work a lot on computers could be a part of an increasing number of digital-age employees who have more than one computer. Whether you work at home or in an office, multiple monitors will allow the person to look at several data streams by shifting an eye.

There are studies that have found that multiple monitors are able to help with productivity. Still, there are experts that think that it will all depend on the work and the characteristics of the person using the computer.

Reiss believes that the psychological effect that multiple monitors have on a person is that they are going to feel more important, which will help their self-esteem, create a sense of respect, and will improve motivation and productivity.

## Diet and Nutrition

Nutrition and diet play a large part in a person's lifestyle. The kinds of food that people eat, how much they eat, and what time they eat factor directly and indirectly into productivity.

Some people argue that breakfast is the "most important meal of the day." Experts think that breakfast will help provide a person with glucose which provides you with energy. Since you can't eat while you sleep, your glucose levels drop and having breakfast in the morning will allow the body to create simple sugars that your bloodstream absorbs where it then heads to the cells for energy.

This is why experts believe that skipping breakfast isn't a good idea since you could lose some valuable productive hours until they eat their first meal.

## Exercise

Everybody knows that exercise can improve your health, but it can also improve your productivity. According to Ingeborg Grabow, "Exercising releases endorphins in the brain." These endorphins are chemicals that your body produces due to some stimuli and can originate in many different areas which include the spinal cord, pituitary gland, and other areas of the nervous system and brain.

According to Grabow, "Exercising four times a week for approximately 20 to 30 minutes is the equivalent of 20 milligrams of Prozac." Exercising also has the ability to de-stress you, it gives you a break, and clears your mind. All of this can boost and increase productivity.

## Physical and Mental Health

How productive you are will often depend on your circumstances and factors like disability and illness. For example, people who have OCD or who suffer from anxiety will often recheck the work they do which can drag out their productivity. Their tendency to become overwhelmed or stressed can hurt their productivity, even if their work is more accurate due to their slower performance. Reiss has broken down the psychological factors that can influence a person's productivity:

*Sincerity* – There are a certain amount of people with antisocial tendencies and overly manipulative people who would see an injury as a chance to misuse and manipulate the disability system.

*Work enjoyment/peer relationships* – People who enjoy what they do and get along with their colleagues will find more motivation to get back to normal functioning. Those who don't like their work or are uncomfortable with their colleagues will often feel taken advantage of. They will see an injury as a way out.

*Family dynamics* – Reiss found that there are two different types of families: those who tend to overreact and overcompensate to a person who is sick or injured and provide more caring and attention than they would normally get, thus creating an unconscious motivation to stay in an injured role, and the dysfunctional family type who reacts in a hostile or negative way to the injured party and view them as worthless or useless. The latter type may sometimes motivate the person to "get better" more often, it will cause them to act defensively to prove that they are injured.

The productivity level of a person can be influenced by several different psychological factors. With the society in the US so productivity focused, knowing the best way to improve it can be extremely valuable and can be helpful to your overall wellbeing and health.

# Chapter 5:
# The Importance of Motivation

Motivation is important to everybody. Motivation helps us live. There is no way to live our lives happily if we don't have motivation. Motivation means that you have desires and purpose to achieve your daily life, business, and career goals. Motivation is what helps us to wake up earlier and be productive.

When we get more than we expect from something, are inspired, or excited is what helps us to become motivated. It inspires people when they read beliefs and stories of those who are successful. It inspires them when they can see a person feel happy and achieve something great. This is how we get motivated and it will end up helping us to reach our goals.

You can find a bunch of motivational things in the world like motivation from teachers, parents, kids, trees, water, seminar, quotes, and books. But we aren't able to find all of them.

The reason for this is because we aren't connected with motivation. Motivation is a sense that is able to reach our mind and heart equally throughout the day, but for a lot of us, we fail to get it. Having a sense of motivation is important to several different life achievements.

**What Is Motivation?**
Motivation is defined as having the will to accomplish something. It works as a psychological force that makes you want to do something. This is a cognition and impression that can end up happening accidentally at any time during the night or day. We get the best amount of motivation when our purpose and motivation meet up. For example, motivational videos can activate your sense of motivation and it will start to connect with your sense of purpose. This is the reason why people will often watch these types of videos and why so many people recommend watching motivational speeches and stories. Motivation will help you to achieve dreams and goals in your business, career, and life.

It can also be said that motivation is the reason or the intent behind something. Why is it that you want to learn? Why is it you like to write? There are reasons behind all of your actions. One of these reasons is going to be a motive.

Another view of motivation is seen in Steven Press field's definition of motivation. He describes motivation as "At some point, the pain of not doing it becomes greater than the pain of doing it." In other words, you will reach a point where it will be easier to change than to stay the same.

This is a very basic definition of motivation. Each choice that is made will come with some sort of price, but when a person becomes motivated, it will be easier for them to handle the inconvenience of taking action than the pain that they will experience if they do nothing.

The funny thing about motivation is that it will often come once you have started your new behavior and not before. Motivation is a normal result of some form of action and not the cause of the action. Getting started on something, even if it is very small, is a type of active inspiration that will provide you with natural momentum.

## Why We Need Motivation

It's important that we have motivation in order to live a flexible, happy, and wealthy life. Motivation will help us to manage our time efficiently. Motivation will help you to manage your daily life challenges, time, and opportunities to help you to move forward and achieve your goals.

Motivation will help you to manage your time and you will become more beneficial and productive for organizations. Here's an example, official, personal dreams and goals will motivate you to wake up earlier. You do yoga and cardio in order to remain fit and healthy. This is because you are working your way towards your goals.

When you feel motivated, you aren't going to want to waste your time. You will communicate based on facts and values. You will be able to focus on the things you have to get done by the end of the day. This is the reason why motivated people tend to be more productive and use their time more wisely.

There are many people who struggle to find their motivation to achieve their goals because they waste all of their energy and time on other areas. If you are interested in making it easy to find motivation and get started on your projects, then you have to automate the early sections of your behavior.

**Motivation Can Make You A Better Manager**
Everybody has been an employee at some point and I'm sure you don't like negative and lazy mindsets in your leaders or managers. This is the reason why motivation in the workplace matters the most for the leaders and managers. The reason for this is that teammates or employees

are able to be less excited to work or negative about projects, but managers and leaders show that they value the project, are excited, creative, and energized.

Motivation will help the business make their employees motivated and happy so that they work hard towards their goals. In order to help increase the motivation levels of employees, businesses and organizations will promote, honor publicly, increase the salary, appreciate, and provide facilities to those who deserve it.

This will help to connect the sense of purpose and sense of motivation in their employee's minds. They will then dedicate hours of their time to achieve the goals of the organization.

This is the reason why motivation will help you to become more productive at work. While there are some employees that can self-motivate and understand when they reach what they are working for, there are people who aren't. If you are in charge of a team of employees, then make sure you talk with them nicely, appreciate all of the efforts, don't focus on their mistakes, and focus on developing them and respecting their feelings and viewpoints.

Never ever make them feel as if they are less than in anything. You should motivate them and inspire them. These motivational practices will improve the morale of your workers and they will find more motivation. This is the reason why motivation within a business is imperative for any form of productivity.

## Motivation in Schools

Motivation is also extremely important for students and teachers. Teachers who are motivated will be able to inspire students to stay focused. Students who are motivated to learn will help to inspire their teachers. Teaching is very much a selfless act.

When it comes to teaching, there is no motivation in the salary. Many teachers in India teach children for free or at a very minimum wage. They don't find motivation in the salary of their job. They find motivation in exploring the creativity in their students. They find motivation in putting smiles on the faces of their students. They find motivation in building their career. They train their students to fight any life and career problems.

Students aren't going to feel very motivated to get an advanced degree when they know that there aren't many jobs for existing degree holders. Teachers aren't going to be very motivated when their government isn't supporting them.

This is the reason why it is so important for students and teachers to be motivated and it's because they are country developers. If these types of people aren't motivated, then you will notice that it takes several more years to develop.

## Motivation in Life

Motivation is important for a successful life. Humans are faced with millions of obstacles every single day. A few of these obstacles are caused by natural disaster out of our control and some are caused by an uneducated society and impractical government laws and policies.

Let's say a farmer's crops are destroyed by flooding then this becomes an obstacle in their life. Their hopes and efforts could disappear. Now the farmer will have to become motivated to try things again and if they don't find the motivation, they won't be able to get things going again. Another obstacle they could end up experiencing is not being able to pay off their bank loan because they are getting lower prices for their crops and so on.

There are many different types of problems and obstacles that we will have to face day after day. Some lose hope and think about giving up.

But when we are able to provide our self with a motivational environment, our sense of purpose will become activated. If we were to attend a motivational seminar or if we read a motivational book, we could increase our motivational environment. If we were the farmer that lost their crops, we could find inspirational stories about others who had gone through the same or similar experience. This would renew our sense of purpose so that we would try again.

*To really live, you have to have the hunger to do so.*

## Motivation in Sports

Why is it that sports players tend to be healthier and more fit than other people in the country? This is because they exercise on a daily basis. The reason for this is because their sense of purpose is strong. They know they have fans and the entire country expecting them to win, and they know that staying physically active and healthy will help them win.

Their motivation for exercising is what others expect from them, their goals, and their desires to reach their dreams, as well as having the hunger to win. This is the reason why motivation is so important.

## Motivation in Nursing

Nursing, similar to teaching, is done with the expectations of a high salary. There may be some that go into for the money, but nursing tends to be a career choice for those who want to help people. It requires heart for a person to be a nurse and care for people unconditionally. It may be a hard work, but for the right person, it can be extremely satisfying for their happiness and soul. With no motivation, it would be extremely hard to stay a nurse based solely on the salary.

## Motivation for Salespeople

Nearly 90% of businesses will give their employees bonuses or incentives for reaching sales goals or creating leads. Promotions, salary, and bonuses have a way of motivating teams to make more sales.

The reason they get motivated is that they get more money once they achieve their goals. They understand that they will be able to use the money they get for their family and personal development. This is the reason why salespeople have all of the motivation they need to sell things.

## Getting A Job

It is possible to get a job offer on the first go, but if you don't, what is going to make you try again. It's a sense of purpose, its reasons, its motivation, it's your desires, and dreams that motivate you to continue trying, trying, and trying. And it's the reason why you keep from repeating your mistakes. You can see this all over the world. People get jobs, work, or projects even after hundreds of rejections.

Life can be very difficult for dreamers. Everybody will struggle and we all do. The reason for this is that we have desires and jobs that motivate us to work through these rough times, and to keeping pushing through to our final destination until we take our last breath. This is why motivation helps people to get a job.

There are a lot of reasons why motivation is important for our daily life, but I think you get the picture. Motivation is what can make you smile and feel happy with your life. Motivation is what helps you to master your skills. Motivation helps improve innovation. Motivation is what helps you to achieve your career goals. Motivation is what helps you make healthy habits. Motivation is what will help you to live a successful life.

## Chapter 6:
## The Impact of Willpower and Self-Discipline

Self-Discipline or willpower is a very important and useful skill that everybody needs to have. It is an essential skill to have in every area of your life, and while most people know that it is important, very few of them will do anything to strengthen it.

Contrary to popular belief, self-discipline doesn't mean you have to be mean with yourself or keep up a limited and restrictive lifestyle. Self-discipline merely means that you have self-control, which shows that you have inner strength and can control yourself, your reactions, and your actions when you need to.

Specifically, self-discipline is the ability to control your behaviors, reactions, emotions, and impulses. It lets you forego short-term gratification so that you can reach long-term gain and satisfaction. It's the ability to say no when all you really want to do is say yes. It doesn't mean you have to lead a boring and restrictive life void of any enjoyment. In fact, it is nearly impossible to be completely self-disciplined in every area of your life. Instead, it could be used to help you focus on what is the most important to you.

Self-discipline is what gives you the power to stick to the decisions you make and see them through without changing your choices. This is why it is important when it comes to achieving your goals. Possessing this skill will enable you to persevere with your plans and decisions until you have reached your goal. It will also show up in your inner strength, helping you to work through laziness, addictions, and procrastination so that you can follow through with anything you want to do.

A common characteristic of willpower is being able to reject the need for instant pleasure and gratification so that you can have a greater gain. This will require spending time and effort to get to it. Self-discipline is one of the key components of success. It can be seen in several different ways such as:

- Trying something over and over again until you have accomplished what you wanted to do.

- The ability to resist temptations and distractions.

- Self-control.

- The ability to not give up even though you experience setbacks and failures.

- Perseverance.

Life will put problems and challenges on your path to achievement and success and for you to rise above them, you are going to have to act with persistence and perseverance and this is going to require you to have self-discipline.

Having willpower will lead to self-esteem and self-confidence and as a result, we lead to satisfaction and happiness. On the other hand, if you lack self-discipline, it can lead to obesity, relationship and health problems, loss, failure, and many other problems.

Possessing self-discipline can also help you to overcome negative habits like drinking, smoking, addictions, and eating disorders. You will also be able to make yourself study more, exercise every day, create new skills, and improve yourself, and grow your spirituality.

As I stated earlier, the majority of people know the benefits and importance of self-discipline, but most of them won't do anything to improve it. However, you can improve this ability just like all other skills. This can be done through exercises and training.

## Importance and Benefits

Having self-discipline can help you:

- Meditate on a regular basis.

- Start a book and finish reading it.

- Overcome the habit of watching too much television.

- Wake up earlier in the morning.

- Continue to work on your diet and resist the temptation of eating foods that are bad for you.

- Head to the gym, go for a walk, or a swim even if your mind is telling you to sit at home and binge watch Netflix.

- Continue to work on your project even after your initial enthusiasm has disappeared.

- Overcome procrastination and laziness.

- Fulfill the promises you made to yourself and others.

- Avoid acting in a rash way or on impulses.

## The Marshmallow Study

## Cure for the Procrastination Puzzle

Over 40 years ago, psychologist Walter Michel, Ph.D. explored self-control in children through a very simple but extremely effective test. He called his experiment the "marshmallow test" and it created the groundwork for our current study of self-control.

Michel and his fellow researchers gave a preschooler a plate that had a treat on it like a marshmallow. The child was then informed that the researcher was going to step out of the room for a few minutes but not before that gave the child a choice. If they will be able to wait for the researcher to return, they would get two treats. If they will not be able to wait, they could ring a bell to call the researcher back in but they could only have the one treat.

Willpower in children and adults can be viewed as the ability to delay gratification. Certain kids have good self-control in order to let go of the immediate joy of eating a treat so that they can indulge in two treats later on. Ex-smokers are able to give up the joy of cigarette so that they can have good health and avoid a higher risk of lung cancer. Shoppers are able to resist the urge to splurge so that they can save for retirement.

Through the marshmallow study, Michel and his colleagues created the framework to explain how humans can delay gratification. He came up with what he referred to as "hot-and-cool" systems that explained if willpower would fail or succeed. The cool system is cognitive and is the thinking system. It incorporates goals, actions, feelings, and sensations. It reminds you why you should wait to eat the treat. The hot system is emotional and impulsive. The hot system is what causes you to respond quickly and reflexively such as throwing the treat in your mouth without thinking about what it could do.

If your willpower fails, it will expose your hot stimulus causing it to override the cool which causes you to act impulsively. Everybody has a different susceptible to these hot triggers. Your susceptibility to emotional responses could have an influence on your life. When Michel revisited the children, who participated in the marshmallow study after they become adolescents, he discovered that those who had been able to wait longer scored higher on the SATs and their parents often rated them as having a good ability at responding with reason, handling stress, planning, and exhibited good self-control in frustrating situations.

It didn't end there. A new set of researchers tracked down the children, now in the 40s, and tested their willpower with lab tasks to see how their self-control was as an adult. Amazingly, their willpower had held up for more than four decades. Those children who hadn't fared well in the task as a child did poorly on the self-control tasks as an adult. It seems that a person's sensitivity to hot stimuli may persist through their life.

They also looked the brain activity in some of their subjects with functional magnetic resonance imaging. They presented them with what was considered tempting stimuli, and the individuals who didn't have much self-control exhibited brain patterns that were different than those who had high self-control. They discovered that the prefrontal cortex would be more active in those who had better self-control. The ventral striatum had more activity in those who had less self-control. Research has yet to figure out completely why there are some that are more sensitive to emotional temptation and triggers and if these types of patterns could be corrected.

Stephen Patterson

# Chapter 7:
# Overcoming Procrastination

It's Friday afternoon and you can hear the clock ticking. You are working like a madman to get a task finished before your five o'clock deadline, while you also curse yourself for not getting started on it sooner.

*How could you let this happen? Where did everything go wrong? Why did you end of losing focus?*

Well, there are all those hours that you spend reading through your emails and checking in on social media. All of the "preparation," coffee breaks, and the time you spend doing other things that could have been left for you to do next week. Does this sound familiar? Well, you're not alone.

Many of us fall into the trap of procrastination from time to time. In fact, according to Piers Steel, a speaker, and researcher, 95% of the population will procrastinate to some degree. While it is probably comforting to realize that you are not alone, it can also be sobering to know that you are holding yourself back a lot.

## Does Procrastination Mean You Are Being Lazy?

Laziness and procrastination are often confused, but they are actually very different. Procrastination is a process that is active. This means that you choose to do something else instead of doing the thing that you know you need to do. In contrast, laziness most often suggests that there is some form of apathy, unwillingness, and inactivity.

Procrastination means that you ignoring an unpleasant but important task, in favor of doing something that is easier or more enjoyable. When you give into these impulses, it can have some serious consequences. For example, minor episodes of procrastination can end up causing you to feel ashamed or guilty. It can end up leading to a reduction of productivity and can cause you to miss out on reaching your goals.

If you procrastinate for a long time, you could end up becoming disillusioned and demotivated with your work, which could end up leading to depression or the loss of your job.

As with all habits, it is completely possible for you to overcome procrastination. The last 12 chapters will each teach you a new trick to overcome your procrastination. But the first thing you need to do is to realize when you are procrastinating. You can have all the tricks in the world to overcome it, but if you can't recognize when you're doing it, they aren't going to be all that effective.

## Cure for the Procrastination Puzzle

You could end up putting off a task because you have had to re-prioritize all of your work. If you briefly delay something important for an actual good reason, then this doesn't necessarily mean you are procrastinating. However, if you continue to put things off indefinitely or you change your focus because you want to avoid completing something, then you are probably procrastinating. You could also be procrastinating if you realize you are:

- Filling up your day with tasks that have low-priority.

- Keep an item on your To-Do list for a really long time even though it is extremely important.

- You read through your emails several times throughout the day without making a decision on what you're going to do with them.

- You begin your high-priority task and then you head off to make coffee.

- You fill up your time with a bunch of unimportant tasks that other people have asked you to do, instead of getting the important things that you have written on your list.

- You wait until you are in the "right mood" or you are waiting for the "best time" to take care of your task.

**Stephen Patterson**

Once you have realized you are procrastinating, try using one of the tricks below to stop procrastinating. You can also use these tricks before you start procrastinating, which will end up saving you time in the long run.

## Chapter 8:
## Figure Out the Reason for Your Procrastination

Earlier in this book, we talked about several different reasons for procrastination. One of the most common questions that a therapist will hear is, "Why do I always procrastinate even though I know it will cause me anxiety?" You know everything that you need to do, but you don't do it or you allow yourself to wait until the last minute to do it. Over and over again you do this. The pattern will continue to repeat. You start feeling caught and trapped in this vortex of procrastination, anxiety, and stress.

A lot of procrastinators have been told or they tell themselves that the reason they procrastinate is that they are lazy, disorganize, or worse, because they don't care. For the most part, there could be nothing further from the truth. Procrastinators tend to be hardworking, capable, and smart people, they just really have a hard time getting things done when they are supposed to and they don't know why.

If you find yourself often wondering about the reasons why you procrastinate, let's take a little quiz to see if any of these sounds familiar. I want you to ask yourself the following questions:

- When you have a task to do, do you start thinking of the different ways that it could go wrong?

- Do you start picturing how all of the important people around you could react if you end up failing?

- Do you find yourself thinking that it's better that you not even try than to do your best and end up failing?

- Do you find yourself overwhelmed by the possibility of your new responsibilities if you end up being successful?

- Do you believe the idea of "If I do well, then other people will expect me to do more"?

- Do you often feel that your success is going to lead other people knowing who the "real you" are?

- Do you think that if you have to do something that you have to do it perfectly?

- Do you often find it hard to persist when things don't end up going just right?

- Would you rather not do something than end up doing it imperfectly?

Your answers to these questions are able to tell you a lot about the reasons behind your procrastination.
For questions one through three, if you answered yes, then your reason for procrastination could be fear of failure. The thought of putting your effort into something but failing creates a feeling of anxiousness, so you decide to avoid doing it. By doing this, when your project does fail, you are able to rationalize that it wasn't really a test of your true abilities, you needed more time.

For questions four through six, if you answer yes, then your reason for procrastination is a fear of success. Procrastination is able to protect you from greater responsibilities and higher expectations that could come along with succeeding. Like the ones who procrastinate because they don't want to fail, you will keep yourself safe from facing all of your true limits by staying away from challenges and putting things off.

For questions seven through nine, if you answered yes, your reason for procrastination could be perfectionism. Because you have the belief that things have to be done perfectly, the result will be that nothing ever gets done. When you have to face a task, you will find yourself becoming overwhelmed and frustrated by your own impossible standards.

While each person's reasons for procrastination will vary, the results will often be the same — an endless cycle of avoidance, anxiety, and shame. You don't ever get anything done and you aren't able to enjoy anything in your life with all of the guilt that hangs over your head. You might play some golf instead of working on the presentation that you need but the image of frowning boss nags at you during your game. You aren't able to relax because you will always have something else that you need to be doing. Procrastination won't work for anybody because avoidance isn't going to get rid of anxiety, it only delays it.

The great thing is that there are many different effective strategies that can help you overcome procrastination and anxiety. By using the tricks in this book, you will be able to learn skills to help you decrease your avoidance and help control your anxiety.

## Chapter 9:
## Audit Your Goals Weekly

If you are really determined to get your procrastination under control and your life in order, then all you need to grab is a sharpie, a few post-it notes, a wall, and a couple of hours of free time. We are going to do what is known as a life audit. This will help you create a starting point for accomplishing things in a timely manner. If you don't know what your goals are, then you won't be able to figure out where you need to start.

An illustrator and writer, Ximena Vennochi detailed the why and the how of a life audit. It's important that you take some time to check in with yourself so that you can see how you are doing, what you are doing, and what has become important that wasn't important in the past. A life audit can help you figure this out.

Basically, a life audit means that you are organizing your life and being completely honest with yourself.

- First, you are going to write down all of your goals, hopes, and life necessities on post-it notes. This could be owning a home near the ocean, getting a new job, or winning an award for your writing.

- Second, you will organize your post-its by category as you start to notice your themes. This could be career, health, family, and so on.

- Third, you will organize them by time. This means how long it is going to take you to accomplish that task.

The really big life audit doesn't have to be done every single week. You can do the big life audit if you find yourself stuck in a rut, every month, or once a year. What you should do every week is to look over the goals that you can do, work towards and accomplish in that single week. Doing this, especially when you feel like you don't know what to do, is a great way to help you accomplish things.

Here's the process:

- Your goal is to write out 100 post-in an hour.

Take your post-it notes and write out 100 "wishes" on each one. These could be any sort of goal or wish that you would like. There is not a single wish that is too big or too small. This could take a while, but brainstorm until you have come up with at least 100 wishes.

## Cure for the Procrastination Puzzle

There are a lot of people who tend to stop at around 30 to 40 post-its. They think they have run out of things that they would like to do or accomplish, and they often feel relieved by that. They believe that the smaller number of goals they have, the more within reach it will be.

If you can really only come up with 30 to 40 post-it, that's fine. Don't be hard on yourself. But I would really like for you to try and reach 100 wishes. This will really let you know who you are. They don't have to be simple things like getting a raise, working out every day, and so on. You need to think big. Think about the places you would like to travel. Things that you have always wanted to do. Have a glass of wine and get creative. You should feel excited about writing these things down because you have likely ignored many of these wants. Now you are accepting the things that you really want to do.

- If you blow past 100 post- in an hour, that's fine. It's also okay if it takes you longer than an hour to write down 100 wishes.

You have now finished your initial brainstorm.

Next, you will sort your post-its and group them into wish themes. Three simple categories could be creative, personal, and professional. This could get a bit confusing as you could easily place every single note under personal. Everything that you want to do should come from some personal place. So, you shouldn't use a personal category. You need to get more specific.

This will likely take you some time to figure out all of your categories. You will probably have to group and regroup until you really figure something out. You may even be surprised by some of the categories you come up with and how many wishes fall into certain categories. Now, if there is a category that you felt came out a little low, it might not mean anything bad. Chances are that category is so close to your heart that you aren't worried about not doing things that fall into that category. It's something that you easily make time for already. At this point, you may need to take a little break because we're going to get more specific.

You will need to plot your wishes by time. You should have a pretty good idea as to what you want and there is probably a lot of stuff going on. You are probably feeling overwhelmed and unsure of where you should start. By sorting these wishes further into a spectrum of when will help to ease this feeling.

When you do this, the category they are in doesn't matter. Some of your goals will affect your life every single day and won't be a onetime thing. Alright, so you have three timeframes you will sort things into:

- Now or Soon – these are wishes that can be done immediately but will need some sort of prioritization or steps.

- Someday – these wishes are long-term goals and milestone moments.

- Always or Every Day – these are wishes that will need deliberate actions that you do every single day.

Now, if you want, you can be more specific with some of your wishes and write a due date. I feel the three categories will be easier for most people to handle than having to get really specific.
Now, look at your categories you found in step two through the lens of your timeframes. Mark each post-it with something that symbolizes the timeframes. You will be able to see things more clearly.

Your priorities should have naturally surfaced. The important thing is to notice if your breakdown aligns with the way you are currently spending your time.

Next, you need to perform your five activities. This means that you need to write down the five activities that you spend the most time on.

Sorting them into a pie chart to represent how much time you spend on each as compared to the others will help you to see where you need to spend your time.

If work takes up a large portion of your chart but you want to make time for other things, then you may want to take work off of your chart. Change your breakdown to show how you spend your time on things you like doing other than your work. This will show you if you are spending the right amount of time in the areas that correlate with your wishes that you created earlier. You may need to rebalance some things.

Now, you have finished your big life audit. This may seem like a lot of work to overcome procrastination, but if you are able to direct your focus on certain goals, you will be less likely to procrastinate.

The next thing you can do is make all of this digital. Put the things you wrote down and the timeframes into a spreadsheet or document of some sort. This way you can pull it up whenever you do another big life audit and compare the results and see how you are faring. Those post-its aren't going to stay on your wall forever.

Here comes the weekly audit. What you need to do is look at your spreadsheet and figure out which goals you are able to do in the following week. Write those down and work toward those for the next seven days.

The next week, do the same thing. See how many goals you accomplished the week before and add new ones for your next week. This will keep you focused and working towards your overall good.

Stephen Patterson

# Chapter 10:
# Get Rid of Negative Self-Talk

Having some self-criticism is okay. It can be a good reality check that will spur you to become better, but there is a big difference between "I need to exercise more" and calling yourself fat.

Too much self-criticism will often backfire because you will start to focus on your "failures" instead of the little things that you can do to improve yourself. Self-trash-talk over a long period of time is associated with depression and stress. Let's look at how to shut up your inner critic.

**1. Place Your Negative Things in A Box.**
You will often blow things out of proportion when you are beating yourself up. The next time this happens, take a few deep breaths and narrow down your negative thought into a tiny little box. Visualize a tiny box and this will tell you that the problem isn't that big and help you to feel more confident.

## 2. Possible Thinking Power.

A lot of people think that they have to think positively. But some research suggests when you are feeling down, thinking positive can make you feel worse. You should try possible thinking. This means finding a neutral thought about something.

## 3. Find Out If You're Really Guilty.

If you accidentally blurt out that your Spanx is too tight, you may think that you have made a fool of yourself, but have you really? Did they all recoil in horror or were they messing with their phone under the table and not paying attention. Ask yourself some follow up questions to figure out how bad the situation actually is.

## 4. Ask Yourself What Your Friend Would Do.

Your friends are your confidants and won't be as harsh with you as you are to yourself. The next time you feel nasty self-talk coming on, think of a person you trust and think about what they would tell you. Also, if you are able to tell yourself something that you would never say to your friend, then you don't need to tell it to yourself.

## 5. Name Your Inner Critic.

A silly name works the best. It's going to be hard to take your inner voice seriously if its name was The Swamp Monster.

## 6.Call Somebody.

Shame can only work if you keep it to yourself. If you have done something that you think was stupid, grab your phone and speak it out loud. This act will cut the shame off at the knees. When you tell somebody about it, chances are, the two of you will laugh about it.

Stephen Patterson

## Chapter 11:
## Focus on a Single Task

Being able to do only one thing at a time is a great way of being very productive. When you think about it, it doesn't make sense. Aren't we supposed to do more in order to be productive? Nope, it isn't. When you do more than one thing is a great way to be busier and it sometimes is a more engaging way to work. When we do multiple things at once, our brains get more stimulated and it will release dopamine which is a pleasure chemical. Studies have shown that even though multitasking is stimulating, it might make us feel productive, but it actually makes us less productive.

The amount of attention that we give to what is in front of us is very limited. Each moment of each day, our brains get flooded with tasks, thoughts, words, sounds, sights, and more. It only has the ability to focus on so much. One study done found that our brains receive over 11 million pieces of information every second but it is only able to process 40 of them. Wow, that is a big difference. We have to learn to invest our attention wisely.

What is even more surprising is studies have shown that when we think we are multitasking, we really aren't. It is not possible for our brains to be able to focus on two things at one time. It is switching rapidly between them. Instead of channeling our energy and focus into just one task, we are spreading ourselves too thin. This keeps us from diving into any of our tasks. When multitasking, we are doing a poor job of everything.

Even though this is true, we can't deny that when we multitask, it makes us feel incredible. This is the main reason we do it. Multitasking will make us less productive in many different ways. Multitasking makes each task longer to accomplish. We can't ignore irrelevant information. It makes it harder for us to organize and store information. It can even affect our memory. When we multitask, our brains automatically go into auto-pilot mode. This makes it harder to remember what we have worked on. This is why when we are watching television with our computers on our lap, we don't remember what was on the television.

## The Drawbacks
There is a lot of evidence that multitasking is very counterproductive. Multitasking being powerful is nothing but a myth. Humans are a single core processor. We cannot take notes, listen to somebody asking for

feedback, and check our emails at the same time. Sure, we can do it, but not effectively. When we juggle tasks, it increases the amount of time we spend trying to refocus on tasks and divides our attention. It gives people the impression that we are focusing on them and essentially, we aren't. It will also rob you of focus that you could be directing toward a more important task.

Hang on, it gets worse. Multitasking can be harmful to our mental and physical health and reduces our ability to make decisions. Multitasking drains our brains and exhausts our minds. It can zap cognitive resources and if it goes unchecked, it can cause us to decreased sharpness and mental decline. People who constantly multitask will have increased level of the stress hormone cortisol and this can damage our memory.

Now, is multitasking still something you would like to perfect? Don't be surprised if you miss goals, make errors, and get burnt out.

## Single-Tasking

This is the complete opposite of multitasking. It is better in every way possible. We might try to resist single tasking because it doesn't stimulate our brains. When we work on only one task at a time, we can go deeper and do the task better. By doing it this way, we aren't spreading our energy, attention, and time among many things. Single-tasking allows us to create more space around our work at any given moment. This allows us to be more creative, make better connections, think deeper, and find more meaning with our work.

If you can remember your last productive day, you weren't doing many things at one time. You were probably working on only one task and spending a lot of time, energy, and attention on it. It will take energy and time to adapt to not being stimulated during the day, but it will be worth it.

Single-tasking even lets us build our attention muscles. This is how much control we have over where our attention gets directed. A study shows that around 47 percent of our time is spent thinking about things that are unrelated to what is in front of our faces. A person who is more attentive will be more productive than a person who only focuses on their work about 50 percent of the time. Single-tasking can help us strengthen our attention muscle since each time we bring our attention back to what we are doing, we are working our attention muscle and this develops our executive function.

Let's compare time with money. You are shopping and you found a shirt and a pair of jeans that cost $20 each. You only have $20 so you can't buy both of them. We can accept this as a basic truth when talking about money, but when we think about time, we can't comprehend the same concept. This is just silly. If two different projects are going to take you two hours each and you need to focus on each of them, we can't do them in the same two hours.

If you think about it, time is more valuable than money since it is scarcer. You can increase the amount of money you get each week, month, and year and many of us do. You can't do this with time. We only have a certain amount in every day, month, and year. Instead of adding time in our days, the best we can do is decrease the amount we take to do the things we need to do each day.

Just like any resource, if we can't figure out how to increase it, our only choice is to manage what we have. This means we have to budget. Yes, I said, budget our time.

We have to diligently track our time just like we track our money. If you are familiar with budgets, before you can efficiently budget, you have to understand your spending habits. When you know where your money is going, you can understand how to manage it. This holds true for time. Many of us have only a vague idea of what happens to our time.

There are apps that help you track your time by client, project, and task. They are easy to use. They will make reports, edits categories, and entries. The best benefit for tracking time is that it will almost immediately stop all distractions. You probably have a mindset that every morning you have to check your social media, email, and wait you need to check on that thing your significant other wanted to buy. When you use a time tracking app before beginning a project, it will be easier to keep yourself focused on just one thing. It will help you stay focused on just one thing at a time.

You will be amazed that you won't be checking your emails constantly. You will begin telling friends, family, and coworkers that you can't be bothered during certain hours. Your focus will increase drastically and you will be moving toward your larger goals.

If you aren't a person who likes using apps, no need to worry. All you need is a timer. Do you believe me that it is that simple? Try it for one week. You need to set a timer for 20 minutes. This is the amount of time you are able to concentrate on a single task before you lose focus. Use this time and only do one thing. Your brain may resist in the beginning but when you have settled into the groove of things, you are going to feel incredible. After the 20 minutes are up, think about how much you were able to accomplish in just 20 minutes. You are going to be amazed.

## Cure for the Procrastination Puzzle

Because we are giving what we do a name and a specified amount of time, we will be more invested in getting it finished. You will spend your time on it instead of letting it slip between your fingers without doing anything. You will be singularly focused on what you are doing when you do it, and then you will see the benefits of single-tasking just because you are accountable for every minute of every hour you work.

Productivity doesn't measure how busy you are or how quickly you work. It is about what we accomplish. This is what we are left with at the end of the day. Doing just one thing at a time is the best way to accomplish more in less time.

Stephen Patterson

# Chapter 12:
# Time Chunking

Do you always have multiple tabs open on your computer? At the end of your day, can you positively show that any task has been completed that was on your task list?

Not to worry. You are among millions of other people that are constantly distracted by all the notifications, alerts, and dings that pop up on all your devices during the day. If you are beginning to feel unproductive by all the things you can't seem to get done, here are some ways to learn how to time chunk to help you stay productive and focused.

## What Is Time Chunking?

A simple definition of chunking is grouping information together in small enough pieces so you can use them efficiently to get the outcome you would like without shutting down or getting stressed. The main source of stress in our lives happen when we feel like we have so many things to do and never enough time to get them all done. We make to-do lists, but then get overwhelmed before we can even start the list.

When we are constantly bombarded with many different streams of information, we can't pay attention to everything at one time. We can't control our memories or go from one task to the next, as well as others who like completing one task at a time.

We will take one task and pull it into millions of pieces or place it together in an abstract whole. Let's say you are on a project trying to do the entire thing at one time, you will become overwhelmed fairly quickly. Just as its counterpart, if you take a project and turn it into a lot of small steps, it will be equally frustrating, daunting, and overwhelming. How can we fix this?

It might be best to learn how to time chunk. By doing this, we are organizing all of our tasks into one so we won't lose productivity or focus when going between tasks. You can organize this by days or hours. You might want to write on Monday and save your social media and email for another day you aren't as busy.

You could also chunk the tasks into hours during your day. If you are in sales, you could take your mornings and do cold calls and your afternoons could be spent answering emails. If you don't know which one would be best for you, try some different variations and settle on what makes you feel more productive. When we say productive, it means the one that helped you reach your goals.

Many people are only able to focus on a certain number of things at once. When a person is learning, they have a tendency to remember things better if they are grouped into groups of three. Groups larger than three are just too hard for us to remember. Basically, we will get overwhelmed after three separate chunks of information.

When we can't reach our goals, it is not because we aren't able to. It is due to the way we focus on the items or the way we are chunking items. When we can take everything that comes at us and put them into ideal sized groups that we can handle, we are helping ourselves accomplish our goals.

## Begin with Capturing

To start the process of chunking, you have to get your ideas out of your head and put them on paper, your cell phone, tablet, or computer. This process is called capturing.

When we keep everything in our minds, we are just adding more stress. We have to create a habit where we write things down that we need to accomplish. We are only humans and can only focus on a certain number of tasks at one time. We can usually handle between five to nine tasks at one time.

Write down the communications, meetings, and ideas you have to do and what you need to do in order to accomplish each one. Write down the tasks that you absolutely have to do. It might be something you want such as that job promotion or other things that are demanding your attention such as taking your child to basketball practice or that laundry that is piling up on the floor. Write down every single thing you have to accomplish this week. Think about this as a dumping ground for all of your thoughts.

## Goals

Time chunking is useless when you don't have any goals tied to your tasks. You need to be sure you know what outcome organizing your time will accomplish. Without knowing, you may just miss the whole point and begin frantically responding to all notifications.

If you react to each thing that grabs your attention, you are not going to be productive at all. You are going to need something bigger to keep you on task. This is where goals come in to play. You need to create goals that relate to completed tasks or money or both. These goals also help guide your plan that helps you reach your productivity levels.

## Planning Chunks

After you have your goals, you are going to want to create tasks in order to help you reach them. This is your plan. If you have a goal of reaching a certain number of sales for this quarter, you will need to work backward and find what activities will get you to that point.

You know what you need to do each day so you can reach your goal. You need to plan your day so your cold calls can be done in the time chunks that were designated for that specific activity. Continue to make time chunks for other tasks like reading and responding to emails.

## Scheduling

Someone once said, "If you don't schedule it, it won't get done." You need to block out times on your calendar for any activity that is important in achieving your goals. This is very important if your work environment has other people who can schedule appointments for you. Place alerts on your calendar to remind you of specific activities that you need to do.

## Get Rid of Distractions

If you have designated a couple of hours every day to write, you have to keep every distraction at bay. Close all tabs on your internet browser and remove your cell phone from your desk so you won't be tempted to check social media or texts. If you have to, let co-workers, family, and friends know that during this time you are not to be distracted.

## Find Common Ground

After you have written down everything you have to do in one week, start looking for what they have in common. Which items are related to career, relationships, or finances?

Chunk these items on your task list that work with the common areas of your life — spirituality, finances, career/work, time, relationships, emotions, and health.

Let's say you are having a problem with your significant other or you forgot your best friend's birthday. You might have a family reunion that you need to cook for, among other things you absolutely have "to do". All of these items can go under the heading of "relationships."

## Tweak and Revisit If Needed

You have tried to time chunk for one week and nothing has changed. You might have failed and didn't get as much done as you used to. No need to worry. This is why we practice self-control. This has to be practiced since it isn't something that can be quickly learned.

If you have always been disorganized, then this approach is going to be very hard at first. Try a couple of things and adjust your time chunking, planning, or goals accordingly. Find one thing that works for you and perfect it until you reach the productivity level you are looking for.

## The Outcome

After you have chunked all your tasks together, you will be able to see the results you want. In the example above, you want to improve your relationships with friends and loved ones. Once you can see the ultimate purpose, instead of having to check off an endless number of items from a task list, you are going to feel less stress and more productive.

When you can begin to think about your tasks as desired outcomes or clusters, you will be able to keep stress away and learn to focus on larger goals instead of getting overwhelmed by tiny details. Why does this happen? We begin to feel inspired instead of being forced to keep going. When we feel inspired, we come up with a better game plan in order to get there.

**Stephen Patterson**

There are many things that are demanding our attention. If we don't make conscious efforts to figure out in advance what things we need to focus on, we are going to live with all the demands at that moment. Being able to focus gives us the ultimate power that will change how we feel, how we think, and what we do each moment of our day. Once we are able to change the way we focus, we will be able to change our lives.

## Chapter 13:
## Reduce Environmental Distractions

Someone asks you what your plans for the weekend are and it might feel like some welcome time off from your busy work week. Time goes by and in 15 minutes, you find out you are late for an important meeting. The stress is back.

It might seem like our places of work were designed to break our focus. Even if you have a bunch of work piling up, you will still take the time to check Twitter, emails, and try to find a cheap flight for vacation even if your manager disapproves. These types of distractions are costly and stressful. It can take around 23 minutes to get your focus back after getting distracted.

The Overload Research Group found that workers in the United States waste around 25 percent of their time trying to deal with incessant streams of data. This loses employers about $997 billion each year.

Let's look at eleven of the most common distractions that we face daily and find ways to deal with them or getting rid of them completely.

## 1. Personal Technology

Smart watches and smartphones have caused the line between professional and personal communication to become blurred. You now get work calls and emails on the same device along with all kinds of personal information, Instagram photos, and private Facebook comments.

Because of technology's addictive nature, trying to implement policies to control them being used during work hours isn't always effective. It is just as hard to enforce rules about what workers can view on their personal devices.

It is better if people can understand and manage these challenges by themselves. You and your co-workers might agree to put away your phones for a specific time throughout the day. This will help you focus on your work.

## 2. Email

Most of the email we receive every day are not important. We have the need to look at them as soon as we get them. Here are some ways to manage these messages so they don't mess up your important tasks.

*Schedule specific times to check:* Turn off your notification alert for emails. Only check and respond to emails at a specified time every day. Give yourself no more than 30 minutes for every set time. Manage your customer's, manager's, and co-worker's expectations about when and how you are going to reply to them.

*Pick times of low productivity:* There will be a specific time during your day when you are at your best. This could be during the mornings or after lunch. Schedule a time to check email during your less productive times and save your peak energy time for work that is very important.

*Turn email into actions:* If it takes you longer than a couple of minutes to read and reply to emails, add them to a task list.

*Use the trash icon:* You don't need to keep email forever. When you do, you could lose sight of the important ones when your inbox gets too full. Your inbox will be harder to manage. After you have replied to them, delete the ones you don't need. Place the ones you want to keep in a separate folder.

*Sync smartphones:* Try to redirect your email to your smartphones. This will help you keep your computers free of distraction. Apply the above device to your own personal devices.

**3.Social Media**

Social media gives us ways to communicate with a huge number of people. It could also kill productivity, breaks our concentration, and takes our attention from tasks that need to be done.

Businesses can't block a person's access to websites that aren't work-related. Smartphones get us around all that since they operate on cell towers that don't rely on work-based internet access. People have to be encouraged to responsibly use social media so their focus and productivity don't get affected.

Try to track your social media activity for one week and jot down the time you spend on these sites while working. Schedule some time every day to answer messages or post updates.

## 4.Instant Messaging

Most workplaces use an Instant Messenger to keep co-workers in touch with each other. It could also be a distraction thanks to emojis and notifications that aren't important. Make a habit of using instant messenger to make fast, small inquiries and not for long conversations. Don't be pressured to reply instantly and set certain times throughout the day to be online.

## 5.Browsing

Ordering things online, checking the latest sports scores, and reading the latest headlines could easily take 30 minutes out of your time. It could also be breaking workplace rules. Turning off the internet isn't an option since organizations are using software that is cloud-based that takes internet connections to work. You could install software that blocks certain websites or any content you don't want to see. If your workplace agrees to it, use a brief personal browsing session to reward yourself for two hours of quality work.

## 6. Phone Calls

When a phone rings, it prompts an urgent need to answer it even if you were in deep thought. In order to minimize this distraction, try to arrange a rotation so co-workers could take the calls of another co-worker. They could use instant messenger to check to see if the person could take the call. If you can't turn off your phone due to family concerns, try to preprogram some fast text replies like — "I'm in a meeting, will return your call as soon as possible." You might try to explain to family and friends that you can only receive a call during the evenings or at lunch.

## 7. Work Environment

Instead of ignoring these distractions like loud co-workers or smelling your favorite food cooking, move away from the distraction. Put yourself in an empty room to gain your focus. Wear headphones that cancel out all noises or play white noise in the background. Whatever it takes to get your attention back.

### 8. Confusion

Try to have a task list that is manageable. If it is too long, it will lead to procrastination as you try to figure out what to do next. Commit to doing the two most important tasks today and save the rest for tomorrow.

If you find that you are constantly dealing with unplanned and urgent inquiries, go deeper and use techniques to uncover their cause. When you address these problems, you can minimize the disruption or possibly eliminate it completely. You are part of a team. Ask co-workers to help with the load when times get busy. If you are the manager, learn to delegate.

### 9. People

If your team isn't a virtual one, co-workers might visit your desk and distract you. If you are a manager, you want to be available to your team members. When you are focusing on a task and don't want to be disturbed, try working from home or in an unused room to avoid interruptions. If you have an office, close your door and let your workers know you can't be disturbed for a specific amount of time.

- If your office has an open floor plan, remove chairs or stand up when a co-worker arrives to make your space not as hospitable.

- If you have a certain person who always disturbs you, talk to them about it. They might not realize they are bothering you.

## 10. You

You need a lot of physical and mental energy in order to juggle priorities, have discipline to control the use of technology, and manage visitors. It is very important that you take time to care for yourself. Most people don't sleep enough due to the distraction of technology in the home. You need to do your best there as well.

Dehydration makes you feel tired and could impact the way you think. You need to drink a lot of water. Get out in nature. Take a walk around the neighborhood. Don't eat snacks with lots of sugar or heavy lunches. This could lead to little or no concentration later on in your day. Researchers have found that you could improve your time management and performance by realizing that some distractions are going to happen and be prepared for them.

## 11. Environmental Distractions

If we aren't invested in our work, we act like crows. This means we try to find all the shiny objects around us to distract us from working. Try to declutter your work and home. Get rid of trash and anything that is a distraction and not practical to your task at hand.

Have two work areas if at all possible. What you use daily should be put in the primary area. Things you use either weekly or monthly can go into the secondary area. Things like staplers, photos, printers, cables, books, etc.

Each object needs to have a place of its own. When you have finished using a particular item, return it back to where it needs to be. This keeps everything organized and you will be able to find every item when needed.

## In Summary

All of us face distraction each day. It lowers productivity and increases our stress. Figure out what causes you the most distractions during your workday. You might find technology will be at the top of the list.

## Cure for the Procrastination Puzzle

Try to create new habits to control these distractions. Be careful with your phone, email usage, social media usage, and messaging usage. Let people know that you don't want to be disturbed. Move away from environments that distract you and find a quiet place to work. Keep your task list manageable and concise. If you can implement these things, it might mean you and your co-workers will get more work done.

Stephen Patterson

## Chapter 14:
## Avoid Being Bored

Boredom isn't caused by not having enough things to do. It isn't even caused by not having things you would like to do. Boredom is often mislabeled to hid different problems. This is the reason why many attempts to stop being bored won't work. They aren't addressing the main problem. Here are some tricks to find the actual culprit behind being bored.

Find out what you actually want to do. Boredom will sometimes mask a problem when you want to do something but another thing is keeping you from it. This might happen when you would like to watch a particular show but your cable is out. If this happens, your first step to kill the boredom is to recognize what activity you want to do.

Get your compass straight. Boredom could be caused by not having a certain direction. Take some time to identify your passions, desires, or goals. At times just thinking about these could get you motivated.

Socialize. Get out of the house and meet up with friends or even make new ones. Boredom might be disguising a need for social energy. Even if you don't know how to meet new people or your friends have other obligations, find an online forum that shares your interests or call a friend.

Learn new things. You might just need some mental stimulation. Here are some things you can do to begin learning new things.

- Write a story
- Research something you are interested in
- Read a book
- Practice your artistic skills

*Get rid of distractions.* Boredom can be created if you are doing tasks that don't mean anything such as watching a show that isn't holding your interest or randomly surfing the internet. Turn off the computer or television and move around until you figure out something better to do.

*Fill up your schedule.* Having too much time is just as bad as having no time. It is hard to adjust to boredom when you suddenly have time on your hands. You might find you get irritated during the holidays when your schedule suddenly becomes empty. Take some time to fill in an empty schedule to keep boredom at bay.

*Be your own cheerleader.* You might be bored because you don't have any confidence. You don't want to work on goals if you have been told you won't succeed. Take time to look at your successes so you can get your confidence back and keep going forward.

*Meditate.* This is a great activity when you have an extreme case of boredom. Check out online sites about how to do it and why it is good for you.

*Journal.* Start a word document and just begin writing. This is similar to meditation but a bit more active and not as imaginative.

*Find a new challenge.* If you realize you are constantly bored, this means you have some time where you don't have anything that will meet your needs. Find a new hobby, challenge, or goal to take up that time.

These are only a few methods that could help you combat boredom. These are only suggestions. The best way to get rid of boredom is to understand why you are bored. Boredom usually has one of five root causes. Figure out that cause and you will be closer to finding a cure.

*Procrastination:* You aren't really bored. You are procrastinating. Find out what tasks you aren't doing and get rid of procrastination.

*Lack of Energy:* Being bored isn't the same thing as exhaustion. It can happen when you have more of one type of energy but are exhausted in useful energy. This happens when you find yourself not wanting to work but you don't feel tired physically. Figure out an activity that will use the overabundance of energy. This might mean you have to do physical things after you have spent your day writing. You may also need to be creative after you have spent the day writing boring codes.

*Schedule Gaps:* You've had a sudden change in your schedule and you don't have a bunch of activities to keep you busy. The answer is to add more tasks. At times you might need to settle into the quiet and use the time to reflect.

*Environmental Obstacles:* Being away from the internet, being on a long plane ride, and standing in line. These examples of boredom force you to become creative until the situation can be changed.

*No motivation:* You don't have any motivation to do what you need to in order to get rid of boredom. For short periods of time, this can be fixed by using some simple tricks. For longer periods of time, you have to address this with some reflection time, reestablish your priorities, and setting some goals.

The first list is suggestions to help you overcome boredom or you could figure out your own after you have found the root of the problem.

Stephen Patterson

# Chapter 15:
# Find an Accountability Partner

When you are making goals and trying to achieve them, you shouldn't overlook how important an accountability partner can be. You could always accomplish more when somebody is beside you supporting, motivating, and encouraging you every step of the way.

**Importance**
You need to think about your accountability partner as a mastermind group. They need to have four pillars — motivating, positive, non-competitive, and intimate.

When you are looking for the right partner, you need to find somebody that has a giving presence and not someone who only thinks about themselves. If you see a partner that helps others without asking for anything in return, they are demonstrating the non-competitive and positive pillars. What you might not know is if they are cultivating a relationship of sharing details about your blog or your business plan.

Try to select the correct personality. Trust is only earned with time. Test the waters before you spill all of your beans. You need to find the right person who believes you are able to achieve your goals in spite of your current problems. This is needed to have success.

## Why A Partner Is Important

An accountability partner will strengthen your why. If you don't know your "why", you need to find it. This will allow you to understand what your goals will look like and keep you on task and help you achieve your goals.

After you know your why, share it with your accountability partner. This will help them understand the reason why you do what you do. They will be able to relate better to you and will be able to remind you about your why when you forget. You might be making the wrong choices and thinking about other people's why instead of yours.

They will show off your strengths. If you have taken time to find the right partner, you will realize that they will be able to see your strengths and encourage you.

They could help you by having you add stuff to your page or even find new areas for you to branch out to help your income.

# Cure for the Procrastination Puzzle

They can see your weaknesses. It won't take long to find somebody's weaknesses. If your accountability partner is perfect, you will feel secure in your relationship. This means when your partner shows you a weakness that is holding you back, you have to understand that they aren't attacking you personally but are trying to help you improve.

When someone shows a weakness, they need to suggest a solution too. This is done to encourage more learning by attending a conference, taking a class, or reading a book.

Accountability partners need to be sounding boards. They are great to bounce ideas off of. This can only be achieved if you trust each other and they have proven their loyalty.

In this world, everyone has things they need to vent about. If you have a blog, try to keep these short and stay away from getting into a long, negative discussion. The purpose of a blog is for growth and positivity.

- You need to look for solutions for problems you are venting about or vent to your spouse.

- Always take the time to celebrate goals and milestones you have reached because these reflect what is necessary and important.

- They will help you set goals. Accountability partners can keep you motivated by setting goals.

After you have decided on your goals and have taken the steps of making goals you need to reach each month, you can hold somebody accountable while they are holding you accountable. Create a social media group that will help you make sure you are keeping up with the daily tasks that will get you to your goals.

They will learn with you. You will learn to love it when your accountability partner is attending the same conference, taking the same classes, or reading the same book. It makes it easy to talk about how to put in into your own success. Figuring out if things are or aren't working is another way to learn together.

They make great mastermind groups. After you know the how, why, when, what, and who of your group would consist of and their guidelines, you can place the four pillars and begin growing together.

# Chapter 16:
# Leverage Your Peak-Energy

Hours are not created equal. At times, one hour is enough time to get through a large project. Other times, one hour only allows you to some of a few emails.

CEOs, performance coaches, and motivational speakers urge you to find and leverage your peak hours as a way to be more productive. If you can learn to follow a schedule that utilizes the work hours when you are more productive, this makes sure your projects get the energy they deserve. Here is a plan to help you harness your power hours.

**Ultradian Rhythm**
Humans run on cycles like everything else in nature. There is growing research about ultradian rhythms. These are cycles that last about 90 to 120 minutes that run in our bodies a 24-hour circadian day. This suggests that each day is driven by cycles that can change how productive and alert we are.

When the cycle starts, we will have more focus and energy. Toward the end, we might begin feeling fatigued and scatterbrained. If your computer is lagging from all those tabs you have opened, you are running in an energy valley.

Having a title of "workaholic" may sound great but that fact of the matter is productivity will drop when you have worked 50 hours or more in only one week. When talking about output, working during your best hours might be better than working longer hours. This is great news.

You need to work during your peak hours when you are feeling excited and alert, especially if your project involves critical decisions, complex thoughts, and problem-solving.

If you try to do these projects when you are in your energy valley, you are going to have to fight with your foggy brain and the project is going to take a lot longer and it will be more painful.

Less complex, unimportant, and routine tasks are easily done when you aren't engaged or focused. When you are feeling sleepy, you could still sit through a weekly meeting. You might have to prop your eyelids open, but who doesn't.

When you know what to do when you have your next surge of energy, you can be assured you will be able to achieve your goals on any given day.

People who are self-employed get to choose the hours they work. There are many companies that now offer work from home options and flexible hours to their employees. There are millions of professionals who have the opportunity to work when they feel productive, inspired, and alert.

All of this sounds great, but it takes us to this question — how can you know when you are at your most productive?

**How Introversion and Extraversion Leverage Your Energy**
You might be wondering what extraversion and introversion are all about. What is more important is how it could help you. Here are a few tips on getting to the root of these buzzwords and some advice on how to leverage your type.

Let's get rid of the misconception that introverts are wallflowers and extraverts are social butterflies. The Swiss psychiatrist, Carl Jung, created these terms. He defined them this way, "The key to finding your style and creating your optimal flow – is understanding where you gain the most energy."

Introverts get energy from their inner selves. This is where their memories, emotions, and ideas live. They feel alive when they research, think, write, and read. Around one-third of the world's workforce is introverted. The funny thing is they might not look like they are.

Extroverts get energy from the outside world. This comes from activities, experiences, and people. They feel alive when they are taking action and engaging externally.

The bottom line is extraversion and introversion are about the energy you get from the stimulation in either your outer or inner world.

**Self-Assessment**
You are probably wondering, "I like to spend time in both worlds. How can I know which one I like better?" The truth is, we all go between the outer and inner world every day.

The key is to find your true style and create your optimal flow. Basically, you need to understand where you get the most energy.

If you still aren't sure, think about doing activities that will either drain or energize you for a whole week. You might find a pattern that specific people or responsibilities are very draining. That is good information to know.

To quote Susan Cain, "The key to maximizing our talents is for us all to put ourselves in a zone of stimulation that is right for us."

Find activities that take you from baseline energy to being purely invigorated. See if they are in your outer or inner world. Commit to watching for the entire period and you might find more energy and focus in one of them over the other.

Now that you can see where you are getting your energy from, leverage it.

### Introverts: Support Your Inner World

*Time to Reflect:* If your boss wants you to brainstorm ideas right now or another asks for feedback, you need to allow yourself some space to reflect by telling them you will get back to them after you have had some time to reflect of their problems.

*Find Private Times and Space:* Wear headphones that cancel out noises. Find time at night for yourself. Find a room that nobody uses at work.

Take time for some one-on-one time with a significant other at home. Give yourself the time you need to get into your inner world without being interrupted.

*Choose to Communicate in Writing:* It is totally fine if meetings aren't your way of getting your thoughts across. Capture your energy and clarity from that inner world by writing email or memos. Writing becomes your support tool when you need to get your thoughts across to others.

## Extraverts: Make Opportunities in Your Outer World

*Have Conversation Offline:* If email exchanges with co-workers feel like they are endless, take the time to talk with them in person or pick up the phone. The answer might come to you in a quick chat or by going on a coffee run. You will get energized with the interaction.

*Work Out Ideas by Talking:* Find a confidant that helps you generate ideas. They are also great to bounce ideas off of. You will go further by this approach.

*Place Yourself Where You Can Engage with Others:* If you have to work on the weekend, try working at a coffee shop instead of an empty office.

## Cure for the Procrastination Puzzle

Get off that treadmill and find a running partner. Create opportunities that put you in environments that will stimulate you more.

Knowing what your energy and communication style is doesn't mean you put yourself in a box. Many people realize they either belong at one end or the other of the spectrum. With time, you will be able to develop a comfortable place so you can step out of your character mode. It doesn't matter if you think you are an extrovert or an introvert, you have to actively identify and find situations that will play to you.

**Stephen Patterson**

# Chapter 17:
# Parkinson's Law

In 1955, famous British author and historian, Cyril Northcote Parkinson said, "Work expands to fill the time available for its completion." This is known as Parkinson's Law. This quote first appeared in the opening line of an article for The Economist. It later became the focus of the book Parkinson's Law: The Pursuit of Progress.

Mr. Parkinson had the qualifications to make this statement because he had worked for the British Civil Service. He had the first-hand experience seeing how bureaucracy works. Bureaucracy is a product of culture because of the limiting belief that we have to work harder is better than being able to work faster and smarter.

The quote "Work expands to fill the time available for its completion". This means if you put a time limit on completing a task in one week that would normally only take you two hours, then this task will get more daunting and complex as the week goes by. You might not even have more work to fill the time frame, but just the tension and stress about knowing you have to get it done causes anxiety. When you assign the correct time for a certain task, you will get more time back and the task won't be as complicated.

Some people think that Parkinson's Law meant that we can give a time limit of one minute to any task and that task will become so simple that we can do it in that one minute. The problem with that is that Parkinson's Law is only an observation and not magic. It works because people will give tasks a time limit of longer than is actually needed. They like having a buffer zone. They don't actually know how long it will take to complete the task. They don't realize how fast certain tasks could be completed until this principle gets tested.

Many employees will defy the rule of "work harder, not smarter". They know that in spite of the better return on investment isn't always appreciated. This is related to the idea that if something takes you longer to complete, the better quality it will be. The rising trend of telecommuting employees is changing for those people who have adapted to this already. Employers don't know what you really are doing with the extra spare time.

Let's see how we can apply Parkinson's Law to everyday life. This will allow you to check off your to-do list faster and won't be spending time trying to fill in time to look busy. This holds true whether or not you work from home or in an office because "work harder, not smarter" is an idea that many people fall into even if their work isn't supervised.

## Run Against the Clock

Create your task list and divide it up by how much time is needed to finish each task. Now you are going to give yourself half of that time to finish the tasks. You have to understand this time limit is critical. It must be treated just like all other deadlines. The only way to reverse what we have been taught about "work harder, not smarter" is seeing the deadlines we've set are unbreakable. These are just like the deadlines your clients or boss has set.

You have to use that need for competition to fuel you just like it does with gaming and sports in order for this to work for you. You have to beat the clock. Beat it just like it was an actual real-life opponent. Don't take shortcuts or produce any low-quality output. This helps if you don't take your own deadlines to heart.

This is going to begin as an exercise to see if you are accurate when figuring out your time projections for your tasks. Some might be spot on and some might be too long. The ones you predicted as spot on might not get met because when you half the time, you actually didn't have enough time. You need to experiment with longer times. Don't go right back to the original time since there might be a better time in between the two.

If you work from a computer, its timer will be useful when you begin this. It will save you some time because the timer lets you see how much more time you have. Using a clock does take some simple math.

## Kill the Cockroaches in The World of Productivity

Find these time fillers such as feed reading and emails that might take you 10, 20, or even 30 minutes. In the productivity world, these are called cockroaches. These pests that don't do anything but make life a pain in the rear. You can't get rid of these pains no matter what you try or how much you try.

Don't allow yourself 20 to 30 minutes to check emails. Instead, give yourself five minutes. If you like challenges, give yourself only two minutes. Don't go back to these tasks until you have completed everything on your task list for the day. After all the tasks have been done, then you can indulge in reading all your emails, checking social media, and feed reading all you want. Spending all your spare time doing these things isn't recommended.

Only about ten percent of these tasks are important. The other 90 percent are totally useless. This makes you focus on the tasks that are important. Just experiment on how much you can actually do in less time. Figure out what makes an email important. Enforce some strict guidelines and create harsh penalties if you slip up. This means using your delete button more.

Experiment with Parkinson's Law and see how far down you can squash your deadlines in all areas of your life. Be aware of the fine line between not enough time and bare minimum. You need to do a job well done in a little amount of time. You don't want to create a disaster that might lose you your job or clients.

Stephen Patterson

# Chapter 18: Prioritize Tasks

You have so much work to do at this moment. Your list is a mess of items and you don't have any idea on how to prioritize them. There are some ways to get your list prioritized without any effort. You can actually apply any of these in just five minutes and know what you need to do next. There have been various methods over the years, with each having their own considerations and quirks.

How do you know what is right for you? Let's look at four ways to help you prioritize your tasks.

**Put Your Tasks into Four Boxes: Important Vs. Urgent**

This prioritization method comes from former President Dwight D Eisenhower. In the year 1954, he was quoted as saying, "I have two kinds of problems: the urgent and the important. The urgent are not important, and the important are never urgent." This quote caused the Eisenhower Matrix to be created. This is a four-box system to organize your tasks by importance and urgency and then doing them.

- The first box will get labeled "Urgent and Important". These are the things you need to do now.

- The second box gets labeled "Important, not urgent." With these tasks, you get to decide when you want to do them.

- The third box gets labeled "Urgent, not important". These tasks get delegated to someone else to do.

- The fourth box gets labeled "Not important and not urgent." These tasks get deleted from your to-do list.

- This Eisenhower Matrix places tasks into two categories and then prioritizes them. It is a quick and easy way to get tasks in order at the beginning of your day.

Action: You need to create a habit of categorizing your tasks quickly by using a checklist like the one below.

### The "Important" Tasks:
- Does it require little effort but gives great results?

- You have to finish this task before others will get done.

- It provides value.

- If you don't complete it, it will affect other projects and people.

## The "Urgent" Tasks:
- If you don't do it, there will be immediate consequences.
- It needs to be done soon.
- You need to give it immediate attention.
- This task is way overdue.

In order to implement the matrix to your lists, use more tags to figure out which box the task will fall into. Once you check this against your task list, you will easily see what is or isn't a priority.

## When Eating Two Frogs, Eat the Ugliest First
This is slightly different from the Eisenhower Matrix. This method of eating frogs looks at your feelings about the tasks on your list.

To quote Mark Twain, "If you eat a live frog each day for breakfast, nothing worse can happen for the rest of the day." The idea is to consume the ugliest frog as early as you can, then the rest of the day will be a breeze. How do you replace frogs with tasks? You put your tasks into four boxes:

- Tasks you hate doing but don't really need to be done.

- Tasks you hate doing but they really need to be done.

- Tasks you like doing and they really need to be done.

- Tasks you like doing but don't really need to be done.

The logic behind this is if you don't like doing the task, it is because it is hard to do. You realize it is important but you just procrastinate. Find the largest, ugliest task done as quickly as possible and the rest will be easy. You can use the tagging method from above for each number to make it even easier.

## For Precise Prioritization, Use the ABCDE Method

This method is a bit more mathematical. It shows that various tasks could have the same priority level. You don't randomly do tasks that have the same priority level as you go down your list. This method creates two different levels of priority. Here is how you prioritize your tasks using this method.

- Go through your to-do list and give each task a letter from A to E. A represents the most priority.

## Cure for the Procrastination Puzzle

- Now, for all the tasks that were given an A, add a number that dictates the order you are going to do them in.

- Continue this until every task has a letter and number.

In order to be sure, you are categorizing them strictly, you have to be hard on yourself. You can't start a new letter until the previous one has been completely done.

If you compare this to the other methods we've already talked about, the A tasks will be the important and urgent frogs.

### Choose the One to Three Most Important

This is the simplest way to get your tasks prioritized. Leo Babura states, "At the beginning of each day, review your list and write down one to three MITs or Most Important Tasks that you'd like to accomplish for the day. That's your whole planning system. You don't need any more than that." This quote is from the book Zen to Done.

If you use the other methods above, you should be able to choose your three most important tasks fairly quickly and be on the path to getting your task list down to zero.

This method totally relies on your very own intuition. Once you have done several projects or get swamped by a HUGE task list enough times, you are just going to instinctively know what tasks are going to be the most important.

At the end of the day, there isn't a true mathematical formula to figure it all out, but there are ways to help you prioritize your tasks and making it a habit. This is a skill you can work on to get things done faster.

# Chapter 19:
# Reward Yourself

You have to set goals and then reward yourself in order to keep yourself motivated to help you succeed. People need to set goals. Yearly, monthly, weekly, daily, and ongoing goals that influence you each day. Some of these goals will be easy. Taking out the trash? Got it. Need to do the dishes? They are done. Some goals can be quite hard to accomplish like trying to have a healthier lifestyle. Why? The main reason the long-term goals are harder is that we can't see any immediate results. You could diet and exercise for months without seeing any changes to your body and it gets discouraging. You need to set goals differently. You need to set goals that come along with rewards.

### The Idea Behind Goals and Rewards
You basically need to set measurable and specific goals that will determine a positive reward when you hit that goal. Here is the main part. You need to keep these promises and reward yourself. The goals need to be challenging and attainable. You need to push yourself to do better

at whatever it is you are doing. Let's say you want to give up drinking soda. You have to set a goal of not drinking soda for two weeks in a row. Your reward is to add money to your new wardrobe fund. The better you do, the more money you will have for shopping. Simple!

## Before You Begin

You might have to get a bit more formal with yourself to make sure you stay serious when setting goals and rewards. Think about creating a contract. Your contract might read:

"I, (your name here), know that I am trying to improve myself every day. I commit myself to these goals, and in turn, commit to rewarding myself appropriately when a goal has been accomplished. These rewards will be fulfilled without restraint or guilt. I, (your name here), commit myself to this self-care for the duration of this contract, a period of six months."

Then you will sign and date the contract. This will add gravity to set the goal. After you have finished this, you will understand the feeling. It will feel powerful and real when you have it written and signed. This should be done before you head into the fundamentals of rewards and goals. This will make you take the process seriously and this is what you want.

## Set the Goal

Your next step will be figuring out what goals you are going to set. You probably already know some aspects of your life you would like to improve. You need to figure out the specifics. You can't set goals that are vague. You need to be specific so you are able to figure out your answer when asked, "Did you reach your goal?"

Setting goals are tricky but can be done. You need to know how to set goals that are challenging but within your reach and that is hard to do. When you do it, it could change your progress. Getting great goals could be the difference between exhilaration and frustration.

To begin, sit down and figure out all the goals you want to set for yourself. Be more creative, drink more water, and exercise more, then think about how you will get to this goal. Try to think about something that if you really tried, you know you can do it even if it is a bit hard. You might want to be more creative, do this task for about 75 percent of the month and the rest you get to do whatever. Track your progress so you can see if you were successful at the end of the month.

## Setting Rewards

Once you have all your goals figured out, begin picking out a reward to go along with each goal. This is a bit tricky. You will want to find something that will lure you to work without hurting the goal. The easiest reward is a treat. Candy isn't a reward especially if your goal is health-oriented since it goes against the entire goal. Try to select something such as adding money to your new wardrobe fund or buy yourself a non-food treat. If your goal is related to creativity, try to find a reward that is also related to creativity that encourages you to continue to practice.

## Find Balance

You might realize that you are playing a dangerous game. It is easy to be self-indulgent and give yourself a huge reward for a task that was too easy. You might decide you deserve a caramel macchiato from that specialty coffee shop on the corner you pass up each day for each week you go without drinking soda. Just one and no more. You don't want to undermine trying to drink less junk. You need to implement some checks and balances. You may need to bring in a third party.

Before you put in ink your final rewards, have it run by your third party. They will be tough and they won't allow you to get ridiculous. They might tell you to tone down the reward or set your goals higher. Having someone you can talk this through with will help you see a different side of you. Having another opinion will work wonders, especially if you can't think of any rewards.

If you don't want your rewards to be money related, that is fine. You could just use time. Give yourself a reward of binge playing your favorite video game. You might not have had time to play your game because you've been so busy. If you have a loving partner, ask them if they would be willing to be a reward. They might be willing to give you a foot or back rub. They might be willing to take over a chore or two like doing the dishes or cooking a meal if you meet your goal. You should be able to find rewards that aren't going to break the bank but still be great motivators. You don't always have to have a financial goal. Find something that is fun and enjoyable.

### How to Feel Motivated?

You will feel more energized to hit your goals when you know there will be a reward waiting for you. You probably work better if there is a threat of lower income, disapproval of a parent, or a bad grade. Because you don't have anyone watching over you, you have to find ways to motivate yourself.

You will find many times that you might be willing to give up on daily goals and then change your mind because you remembered your reward. That treat might illuminate that light ahead on rough days. Don't forget to show yourself some love and set those goals and rewards. You will be able to accomplish your goals if you just keep the right attitude. The main attitude you need in order to succeed is to tell yourself that "You deserve good things." You absolutely do deserve good things, everyone does. You just need to get out there and grab them.

# Chapter 20:
# FAQs

**1. What Does It Mean If More Than One Type of Procrastination Relates to Me?**

There is no reason to panic. They are all human traits and it is normal for anyone to be able to identify with all of them. There may be one or two that might jump out at you. The six types represent the outer opinions of three traits:

Attention to Details: A perfectionist will pay too much attention to little details. A dreamer won't give it enough attention.

Focused on the Future: A person who worries is overly concerned about what could happen if.... A person who creates crises isn't concerned enough until it is down to the wire.

Relating to Others: A person who likes to defy will always go against what other people want. A person who pleases understands what other people want.

## 2. Why Is It So Difficult to Change Procrastination?

Procrastination gets driven by tenacious personality traits and strong emotions. Therefore, it makes it hard to change. If it was simple like making New Year's resolutions or by just doing it, your teacher's scolding and mother's nagging would have cured it many years ago.

In order to change a habit, you have to put into place certain strategies and skills that work with your personal style. This is necessary since advice for one type would be completely wrong for a different one.

## 3. Everyone Procrastinates, Don't They?

Nobody is perfect. Procrastination will happen. Your closet continues to be messy even after you promised yourself you would clean it. Holding a tough conversation gets delayed until you have no other choice. The response to a certain request will go unanswered.

For many people, procrastination isn't a thing that happens every now and then. It is a deeply rooted, pervasive, and chronic pattern. If you are like this, you know you tend to allow things to slide. Not just the hard tasks but with the easy ones.

## 4. What Is Procrastination?

We are all the time veering around procrastination. So, what does it mean? Some think it is just laziness. This is so not true. The truth of the matter is procrastination is an approach/avoidance conflict that was never resolved.

There is a part of you that knows you need to do a specific task but other parts will keep you from doing it. You are constantly torn between two conflicts. To quote Hamlet, "To do or not to do." I know that it isn't the right quote but it gets the point across. Being indecisive makes it hard for you to be able to choose a commitment to action.

## 5. Why Does the Digital Age Make It Harder to Beat Procrastination?

Addictive, appealing, and accessible distractions are everywhere you turn. Social media seduces. Digital devices deter. Entertainment always entices. Diversions are around every corner. Cell phones constantly chatter. If you take the time to add up the time you spend on all the things that don't have anything to do with your career or personal goals, does it really shock you that you are teetering on the edge?

## 6. What Do I Do If I Know Someone Who Could Really Use Some Help with Their Procrastination?

**Stephen Patterson**

Get proactive. Purchase this book and give it to them as a gift. You are probably as frustrated watching them as they feel. It is hard watching your family and friends not doing as well as you know they can. Tell them you hope this gift will help them achieve the success they deserve. Now take a step back. You can't do it for them. You can only provide them with the resources they need in order for it to happen.

# Conclusion

Thank you for making it through to the end of Cure Procrastination and Become Productive. Let's hope it was informative and able to provide you with all of the tools you need to achieve your goals whatever they may be.

Procrastination will get you nowhere. You will end up feeling stressed, anxious, angry, and any other negative emotion you can think of. Quit this evil cycle today. Use what you have learned in this book to turn your life around for the better.

**If you find this book helpful in anyway a review to support my endeavors is much appreciated.**

**Stephen Patterson**

# Successful Habits of Extraordinary People

Develop Over 7 High Performance and Effective Atomic Habits - Blueprint to Powerful Stacking Habits that Stick and Mini Habits to Achieve Any Goal

Stephen Patterson

## Introduction

It may come as a surprise to learn that there are very few traits that separate the average person from the utmost successful people. In this book, we are going to discuss many topics that include: developing effective habits, which habits to stick to, the accumulation of habits, keystone habits and taking action, the secret habits of the successful, keys to financial success, keys to social success, and stacking habits. Most importantly, cover the characteristics of the successful and how they maintain their success. These are surprisingly simple and straightforward habits that virtually anyone can apply to their everyday. Whether you want to be a world-famous astrophysicist or improve your finical situation to finally losing weight and staying slim for years to come. The key to tackling any goal is having the habits to develop a mindset to do so.

As you can tell by now, there will be much emphasis placed on the formulation and maintenance of habits. This is because it is ultimately our habits that make us what we are, and if these habits are not healthy and productive ones, then we cannot expect to be healthy and productive people. The role that habits have to play in our everyday lives is not to be understated under any circumstances. If you want success in any given way, then the habits that you form are going to be the most critical factors in obtaining successes or achieving your goals.

We also discuss the keys to financial and social success within this book. When most people think of success, they tend to picture wealth and luxury. While this is not the concept of true financial success, we are still going to delve into what is. Social success is what most people are really after in life, even though people tend to focus more of their energy into achieving financial success. This is why we are also going to delve into some of the secrets of gaining social success to be more highly regarded among your peers, and your self-esteem will be bolstered.

# Chapter 1:
# Developing Effective Habits

It is always amazing the role that micro-habits have to play in the fostering of long-term success. People tend to wait around for magic beans when it comes to success rather than putting any hard and, more importantly, extended work into whatever it is that they are doing. They let their judgments cloud their thinking with delusions surrounding their success. It is the multitude of small steps and habits that lead to success more so than large gestures and the bets made on chance happenings. The issue that most usually face is that they put all their faith in the latter and none in the former—this leads them to make little to no progress though, as it is always the small things that accumulate to give you your successes in life.

You can look at your future like it is something that you have no control over and like it is something decided by fate that does not stop to consider any of your efforts, or you can look at your future like it is something that you can take measures to control. Thinking of it through the lens of some predetermined fate is rational because there are ultimately a lot of happenings and situations that are inevitably going to be out of your control. This is a realistic and true proposition to put forth and to accept it is part of being a grounded person. You can, however, also look at your future through the lens of a time that is more adaptable and more flexible based on what you want to do with it. This mindset is more what we would call a growth mindset, as it allows for more personal growth than does the other. Thinking of your future this way will give you much more power over your fate. If you believe that you are just being tossed about randomly by the world, then you have a much higher probability of just being tossed about randomly by it. Successful people, on the other hand, take the initiative in what they do and are usually rewarded with more control over what happens to them. To use a platitude that is thrown around very often these days, they go out and happen to things rather than sitting around letting things happen to them.

Again, the role that little habits that have to accumulate over time have to play here is never to be understated. One way to better gauge your production of these habits is to do so quantitatively. For example, let's say you make a 1% improvement on a skill every day for a year—that is a dramatic 365% improvement that you have then made by the year's end. How did you come to that? It is by small and incremental improvements that built themselves upon one another over time. It would be more or less impossible to have made that drastic of an improvement had it not been for you practicing the skill every day or, in other words, developing habits that enabled you to make such improvements.

The central concept that makes small, everyday habits so important is the concept of compounding interest. The choices that you make from day to day may not have very noticeable effects within a more limited timespan, but their results tend to accumulate over time. In other words, they "compound," causing more substantial effects—either positive or negative.

This can, however, be a bit of a double-edged sword because bad habits that develop can also have a way accumulating in their adverse effects. For example, if you go to a gas station every day and buy a can of Coke, you are going to be more likely to have a health complication at the end of the year than you would if you had bought a tea every day. Again, the effects of your everyday decisions here compound over time to lead to even more significant consequences. If you make good choices, you will see good results—if you make bad decisions, you will see adverse effects.

We tend to be more outcome-focused than we are process-focused. This is especially true in today's world, where everything that we could ever want is already given to us on a silver platter by technology. This causes us to overlook the means by which things are produced and procured. Looking for outcomes without first learning the methods by which these outcomes are created is an excellent example of wanting to know without wanting to learn—or expecting your reward without putting any work into what you are doing. These are attitudes that are all too common in today's world, but those who avoid falling for these traps see many gains for doing so.

Two of the most important hallmarks of compounding interest are the plateau of latent potential and phase transition. The plateau of unrealized potential is the period in which you are making improvements and forming new habits, but are still not seeing any results for doing so. This is a period which naturally frustrates many people because it is hard to see any effects of one's own efforts throughout this time. This plateau is, however, punctuated by another period which goes by the name of phase transition. In the phase transition, you start to see some reward for all of your efforts. When graphed this period looks like the beginning of the curve of a hockey stick. This is your delayed reward for the effort that has accumulated, and once this phase transition is met, you can then expect good things to happen in your efforts in the future. There is a brief apprenticeship period for your growth in what you do, but once this bottleneck is squeezed through you will come out of the other end with new skills at hand and new possibilities for further improvement.

Before you can reach this phase transition, however, you must first establish skills in mapping out what habits you are going to pick up. When you first start developing new habits, your progress may prove to be so slow that you feel like you are not making progress at all, or even making negative progress. This is because any rewards that you are going to reap from your newly established habits are going to be delayed and are not going to seem very important at first. It is only after sticking to these habits for a more extended period that you will see any results.

One of the most natural and most effective ways of developing new habits is by adjusting your environment according to what habits you want to build and what habits you want to get rid of. This is done most effectively by increasing the number of steps it takes for you to indulge and bad habits while at the same time decreasing the number of steps that it takes for you to develop good habits. Let's take TV for example. This is a destructive habit, so you would want to increase the amount of effort it takes for you to watch TV on a whim. This could be done by taking the batteries out of your remote and only putting them back in when you want to watch TV, which would add some seconds to the process of starting to watch your programs. You could also leave the TV unplugged until you know the name of the show that you want to watch. This would prevent you from watching TV absentmindedly with no real aim at what you are watching in particular. This would be an example of increasing the number of steps involved in indulging in a habit that is bad for you. An example of decreasing the number of steps it requires to develop a habit that is good for you would be keeping a book on your bed stand. This makes the book more readily accessible to you than would leaving it on your bookshelf.

To be human is to err, so you cannot get discouraged when you do not make the marks that you set for yourself. You are going to make mistakes in whatever you do, so all that you should ever try to control is the number of errors that you make. You can do this by going back and analyzing what lead up to your mistake, and then applying the lesson that you have learned to your further efforts in the future. The important thing here is to keep moving on in your efforts no matter what happens. If you do not stay on top of your progress, then your mistakes are bound to multiply and increase in frequency.

## Stephen Patterson

The next point that we should touch on is the learning curve. Once you master a skill, your fluency in that skill reaches a position on the top of a bell curve and usually stays there unless you neglect to keep developing your craft. There is, however, also something called a forgetting curve, which predicts the lessening of skill and the forgetting of its components. This can be caused by not staying on top of your practicing and positive habit forming. Once this starts to occur, it is easy to lose a lot if not all of the skills that you have developed through your new habits. Once a new talent is developed it requires constant fostering and improvement to retain.

After new habits have been developed, new routines and rituals start to emerge. You can think of habits as the microcosms in these systems and methods and rituals as the microcosms here. Your habits become the building blocks for your larger routines. If you create and develop more efficient habits, then you are bound to produce more efficient methods eventually.

To build entire routines and rituals out of your habits, you must first master the art of doing what you do every day. This can often take more effort than learning the habit in of itself can, but once you get into the habit of practicing doing what you want to do every day, you will start to see lots of improvements in your performance. All too often, people get to focus more on the outcome of their goals more so than they do the means by which their goals need to be met. Getting exposed to what you do each and every day is the only reliable way to get a grasp on what you need to do to achieve your long-term goals. If you are not in the regular habit of practicing whatever it is that you need to practice every day, then you cannot expect to learn what it is that you need to do to produce what you want to.

One truism that always applies to you no matter who you are or what situation you find yourself in is that no matter your current life situation, your existing systems of habits cause these directly. The things that you do and how you act are the only good indicators of how your life is going to go. If you want to match an ideal that is different from where you are at currently, which you always will, you then have followed the steps laid out for doing so. Start by analyzing whomever it is that you look up to and then follow in their footsteps. An all too common mistake that most moderns make is neglecting to accept the fact that they have things to learn from other people. You can ultimately listen to what a person has to say in one of two ways: as you know more/better than they do or like you have something to learn from them. Listening to others in a second way will always get you further than will the first way.

### Stephen Patterson

Ralph Waldo Emerson once said that "A man is what he thinks about all day long." You embody the things that you want to be every time you focus on doing those things. If you spend an hour everyday writing, you are playing the part of the writer in your own life for an hour out of every day. If you keep on top on your laundry and your dishes every day, you are embodying a tidier and clean person. The same is true for bad habits though. If you smoke a pack of cigarettes a day, you are representing a smoker throughout that time. If you watch TV for an hour a day, then you are embodying a TV viewer throughout that time. You can never expect to become good at something if you never spend any time representing a doer of that particular something. When you start to perform the tasks of those whom you want to be more like, then you will begin to cast votes towards your being more like those people and developing your own skill sets. In the end, you reap what you sow, and you will always wind up being worth about what you put into your skull. If you fill yourself up with junk, you are going to get the junk out. If you fill yourself up with gold, you are more likely to get gold out.

The hard thing to grasp for many people when it comes to goal setting is the fact that meeting the end goal that you have in mind is never really the critical part. What is more important is your evolution throughout the process. This is another reason why establishing productive habits is so important. It allows you to gain tools for meeting any goals so that the original purpose that you have in mind will be just one of many to come. As cliché as this may sound, it is always more about the journey than the outcome. For example, if you want to get rich would you instead do so by winning the lottery or by spending countless hours doing work that you love? Most people would choose to win the lottery, which is where most people are wrong. Let's say you win the lottery and wind up with the same skill set that you have right now. Your life is not going to be better than the version of yourself that earned that amount of money through hard work and developed too many skills to even measure along the way. The path to happiness is virtue, not pleasure. Likewise, the road to success is hard work, not blind luck.

Another essential aspect of habit performing is identity building. It is much easier to stick to the habits of something or someone that you identify with. If you identify as a pianist, for example, you are going to feel much more inclined to practice the piano regularly and developing the skill is going to feel a lot more natural to you. Once you establish a firm identity as to what you want to be, you start to build confidence in your abilities, and you then begin to develop skill more effectively.

When it comes to behavioral change, one of the most important things that you can do regarding outcomes is to make your results seem as satisfying as possible. Research suggests that behaviors that provide immediate reward tend to be performed very often, while actions that provide delayed rewards tend to be avoided. This is very unfortunate because often behaviors that offer immediate rewards wind up not producing very many great things in the long run. So, as you can see, most people avoid decisions that will benefit them in the long term. This can work to your advantage if you keep in mind to take advantage of the things that are more likely to give you better long-term rewards. If you get into these habits and avoid the habits, which only provide you with short-term rewards, then you will start to see more results further on down the line than you would otherwise.

You can better assure that you are developing habits that will give you more long-term rewards by supplementing these habits with short-term rewards. For instance, if you want to get in better shape, you could give yourself a pass to eat an ice cream cone whenever you go to the gym. This will trick your mind through classical conditioning into believing that you are getting an immediate reward for doing something that will only give you a long-term reward.

Another, and usually more effective, way of rewarding yourself in the short term for decisions that will benefit you, in the long run, is what is known as identity reaffirmation. This is the practice of reminding yourself that you are the type of person who is more inclined to do x, y, and z. Every time that you read a chapter of a book, for example, you can then take a moment to remind yourself that you are the type of person who reads a lot and that you are brilliant. This can be a better method of rewarding yourself in the short term than external rewards can be because it offers a more profound reward, that of heightened self-esteem. If you are reaffirming the identities that you want to take on in the actions that you perform, then you will be more likely to stick to your own goals and habits in the future.

Again, so much of success depends on the little habits that you have. The only way to change your life effectively is to take incremental steps towards your goals by adjusting the habits that you have accordingly. Taking these steps will beset you on all sides with all sorts of issues, but they will also help you succeed in whatever it is that you want to do in your future.

## Chapter 2:
## Which Habits to Stick To

When we delve into all of the habits of the most successful people among us, we invariably start to see some common themes among them all. In this chapter, we will discuss some of the most common habits of the most successful people in our culture and which ones will bolster your chances of success in whatever it is that you do. We will also take a look at some of the most detrimental habits people develop and why you should avoid some of these.

To start with, the most successful people among us read almost regularly. You cannot expect to learn anything about whatever topic it is that you want to improve on without reading up on the subject. It is also true that overlearning will lead you to much better results, in this case. Hence, the more that you read on a topic, the better you will become with regards to it. This is just common sense, but so few people read up on whatever it is that they are interested in.

## Successful Habits of Extraordinary People

All in all, Americans read a mean average of 12 books a year, which is more than some might expect. The median average, however, is only around 4. Around 88% of the most successful people in America read for at least 30 minutes every day.

We should now look into some math involving these reading statistics. Let's say you read for 30 minutes every day for a year. Going at a rate of one page per minute (which is feasible when reading most average-sized books) would put you near a rate of 30 pages per day. Learning at this rate for this amount of time would put 10,950 pages under your belt within 12 months. The average length of a book in pages is only around 300 pages, so you would read on average 36.5 books a year reading at this pace. Now, imagine if you were to limit yourself to just one or two subjects in all these readings. You could most likely become a leading expert in at least your community on whatever these subjects are. With that, you have just given yourself the same amount of readings that most college degrees on the issue would require just by avoiding the TV trap that most people usually fall for at least 30 minutes a day. Reading is not only incredibly entertaining and informative, but it is also one of the most excellent time management techniques that you can employ.

Another thing that the successful do that most of us tend to overlook is meditation. Meditation will help clear your mind from the many stressors that plague you every day. Upon beginning to get into the habit of meditation, you may not see very many results. However, once you practice meditation techniques, you will start to see more clarity in your thinking and gain much more energy for other tasks. Meditation will also improve your memory and make your decision-making processes much faster—it even boasts many physical benefits, such as decreased blood pressure and stress levels.

As you can probably imagine, developing a new skill is usually much more complicated and multifaceted as a process than it might seem at first. No matter what you are trying to improve on, there are always many different sub-skill sets that need to be put in place to do so. This will leave you feeling overwhelmed at times, which is precisely why meditation is so essential. Meditation allows you to drop everything that you have to focus on at a moment's notice. Becoming accustomed to doing so will make you much more relaxed in regards to how many things you have on your plate. You will see more clearly what the steps are that you need to take to move forward towards your goals. Dropping all of your problems for a brief amount of time gives you a new perspective on them. It allows you to look at all of your issues analytically rather than synthetically. When you do this, you stop seeing all of your problems as being part of one big burg of questions, and you start to better hone in on just what exactly is wrong in every scenario and how to fix it.

Meditation often gets a reputation as being an egg headed activity meant for yogi masters and soccer moms, but you cannot underestimate its value in improving your cognitive functioning and overall physical health.

Another important thing that the most successful among us do is waking up early. Around 50% of the wealthiest people in America claim that they usually wake up around 3 hours before their workday starts. This gives them lots of time to complete side projects, plan out the day ahead, or workout. Waking up earlier gives you an advantage because you are getting to the "meat" of the day earlier than others are. Your peak logical reasoning throughout the day occurs during the morning hours, as does your peak libido. If you are not doing anything while these occur, then you are missing out on a lot of the productive benefits that these peaks have to offer you. Taking advantage of these higher levels of cortisol and the benefits that come along with this will help you achieve your goals much more effectively and efficiently.

One of the main things that people often do wrong (usually out of necessity) when it comes to waking up in the morning is, they wake up right before they have to go to work. This makes their thinking foggy and their judgment unclear when they first start their days off. It is always better to lengthen the time between your waking up and your starting work as much as possible. Do not start working 4 hours before bedtime, but you should also avoid practically waking up at work. Your brain needs time to wake up before you get into doing your standard routine.

The successful also sleep a lot. Albert Einstein, for example, always insisted that he need at least 10 hours of sleep a night to perform at his best capacity. Around 89% of the wealthiest Americans are reported as sleeping 7 to 8 hours each night. Sleeping is not only a performance enhancer when it comes to routine work, but getting adequate amounts of sleep also has very many physiological benefits as well. Neglecting to get enough sleep can cause many adverse health complications. Memory issues are among these. Sleeping helps your brain to make connections and to process and store information that it would not otherwise save. A lack of sleep can cause a decline in all types of your memory, including both long and short term.

Another effect that sleep deprivation can have on the body is mood changes. In the short-term lack of sleep can make you short-tempered, moody, and or emotionally turbulent. In the long-term effects on mood can be even more severe, ranging from anxiety and or depressive disorders, to paranoia and even psychotic disturbances. Another cognitive impact that a lack of sleep can have on you is trouble thinking and or concentrating. The connections above that your brain makes during sleep also foster problem-solving skills, creativity, and concentration. Without adequate amounts of sleep, you cannot expect any of these skills to be up to par throughout your days.

Another effect of sleep deprivation is the increased risk of accidents. Performing tasks, while you are drowsy, makes it much more likely that you are going to run into crashes while doing so. Sleep deprivation also weakens your immune system as well. This can lead you to be more vulnerable to catching illnesses that you otherwise would not have caught. You will be more likely to get sick when you are exposed to germs. High blood pressure is another adverse consequence of sleep deprivation. Statistics show that those who sleep five hours a night or less increase their risk of developing high blood pressure dramatically.

Diabetes is another disease that you have a better chance of developing if you are sleep deprived. Lack of sleep leads you to imbalances in insulin levels which can affect your blood sugar levels and increase your risk of developing type 2 diabetes. You also tend to gain much weight when you are sleep deprived. This is because the chemical messengers that are sent from your stomach telling your brain that you are full cannot work correctly when you are sleep deprived. The result of this is that you are more likely to overindulge yourself in what you eat and you, therefore, put on extra weight.

Your sex drive is another important thing that is affected by lack of sleep. Lack of sleep can cause lots of endocrine imbalances which can have adverse effects on your sex hormones, primarily testosterone in men and estrogen in women. These imbalances can cause your sex drive and your libido to lessen. Moreover, finally, poor balance can also be caused by a lack of sleep. This can make you more prone to falling and other accidents.

As you can see, an adequate amount of sleep is not only a prerequisite for success, but it is also a prerequisite for healthy living in general.

Another behavioral trait of the hugely successful is exercise. The successful do not just go to the gym to gain muscle mass. They do so to retain their overall health. Not only will exercise help your body to perform its regular functions, but it will also help your mind to perform better. Your brain requires copious amounts of oxygen to complete all of its duties regularly. Exercise will help you get enough oxygen to your brain, which will then increase your cognitive functioning. Not only will exercise keep your IQ from dropping below what it is at, but it will also improve your memory and learning abilities. Around 76% of the wealthiest Americans report that they spend at least 30 minutes a day biking and or running. This helps their bodies and minds to continue performing their normal functions.

The most successful among are always improving their communication skills. Not only are they great and clear communicators, but they are still trying to improve on this trait with nearly everyone whom they come into contact with. This makes them ready at a moment's notice to discuss more important topics reliably and straightforwardly. Spending all of your time learning things is not likely to do you much good if you are not relaying these ideas to others. After all, what good are your ideas if all that they do is stay within your head? No one can get any value out of the things that you never say. While it is essential to know what it is that you are talking about and be careful and precise in what you say, it is ultimately more important to communicate your ideas with others so that people know what you are thinking. Working on your communication skills can be one of the quickest means of improving your overall quality of life because those around you can immediately know what you want them to know. It is amazing how quickly people will be more receptive to what you have to say if you start throwing more and more of it out there. This is especially important for shy people to keep in mind. Do not be timid in what you have to say. So long as you speak to other people with respect and confidence, everything should go relatively well.

Successful people also talk to themselves quite often. This is a great way to improve your communication skills when no one else is around. This method also allows you to get a better grasp of what you are thinking about something that you are aiming for. You can better organize your thoughts regarding a topic when you write some of your ideas down and or relay them to yourself verbally. This will make your dreams more transparent and more memorable to you, and it will also make adjusting those thoughts to be more rational and useful a lot easier. You cannot expect all of your plans to follow through if you are not introspecting on them in this way.

A big factor in the merits or demerits of your communication is your ability to build your internal dialogue effectively. Mastering your internal discussions will allow you to come into conversations regarding your plans with more confidence and more effectiveness. If you go into a business meeting just ad-libbing everything that you have to say, you cannot expect to achieve the same results that you would have had you came prepared in what you have to say.

There is yet another benefit in talking to yourself that should be touched on here. Talking to yourself about things allows you to analyze specific situations with more objectivity and more rationality than you would otherwise have. You are better able to interpret what exactly you are saying when you are saying it in a way that you can hear and not just think. This allows you to put greater checks on yourself to keep yourself from just running away wildly with whatever ideas that pop into your head.

The next method that the successful use is closely related to the last one, they journal each day. When successful people do this, however, they do not just vent or aimlessly write down whatever is on their mind. Instead, they focus on their future goals and plans to achieve those goals. This is a much more reliable method of sticking to goals than just thinking about them mentally. Once you put your ideas into writing, they crystallize into something much more concrete. You are giving yourself a real, tangible starting off point in writing down your future goals. Journaling can also be an excellent means of self-care therapy. You can focus on what your problems are that you need to solve as well as what your goals are. This can help you better understand what bothers you the most and how to explain the most problematic motifs in your everyday life.

The most successful among us are also the least fearful among us. This is not to be confused with the avoidance of things that make us afraid in practice though. It is not that the successful need to avoid scary things, it's that nothing really scares them and, therefore, few things hold them back. So many of the barriers that we see before ourselves are placed there by fear of what we have yet to see. The only way to break these unnecessary barriers down is to face the things that we fear the most and to break free from the self-imposed shackles that we often find ourselves in. A lot of the times the fears that we are harboring are caused by past events which occurred long ago in our pasts. These fears are particularly harmful because they are often entirely divorced from our current reality and therefore do not help us with our current problems. It requires close thought tracking to determine which fears you have that are helping you and which ones are hurting you. Once you gain skills in doing this though, you will reap great rewards for doing so.

The successful are also more inclined to step away from their devices than the rest of us. This allows them to keep a clearer head than the rest of us do. Taking time away from your TV, smartphone, and or laptop will help you feel more natural and saner. You will also lessen your dependence on these things by doing so.

To be successful, you must keep yourself grounded as much as possible. It is all too easy to let moderate successes go to your head and to start slacking off because you believe that you are already ahead of everyone else. This is a wrong approach to take because, firstly, it is impossible to stay ahead of everyone and, secondly, you should never be comparing your success to that of others, you should instead always be comparing yourself to the person who you were the day before, with the aim of always being a little bit better than that person was. You have to check your pride at the door and admit that others may know more than you do at times to move forward.

Another trait of all of the most successful people among us is persistence. You can never expect to achieve any of your goals if you do not practice perseverance and self-discipline. It is, after all, only small and incremental steps that will get you to where you want to be when you are trying to achieve a particular goal. The adage "slow and steady always wins the race" holds here as anywhere. It is always smarter to try to accumulate your efforts and take steady steps towards the completion of your project than to expect to complete the entire thing within one day. You cannot write a symphony of any worth within 24 hours (unless you are Mozart), so instead, you need to get into the habit of working on what it is that you love to do each day.

Above are the most common characteristics that all successful people have. As you can already tell, these traits take time and energy to develop, but once you start to practice these traits, you will see great results in whatever it is that you enjoy doing.

## Successful Habits of Extraordinary People

# Chapter 3:
# The Accumulation of Habits

As we have already gone over, the effects of small habits tend to accumulate and grow over time. Now, we should go over just how these effects can grow exponentially, why this is important, and how to maximize your benefits from this phenomenon.

We should start with some basic math. Let's say you get 1% better at performing a task each and every day for a year. This means that at the end of the year, you will be 36.5% better at performing the task. The equation for this looks like this: $0.1 \times 365 = 36.5\%$

You can, of course, adjust your workload based on just how much progress you desire to make and just how much time you have on your hands. If you wanted to get 10% better at performing a task, for example, then you would need to practice it for 232 days in a year under this model. This equates to 5 days per week, which is much less intensive than doing it every day.

Now, we should analyze why it is that some habits are more comfortable to stick to than others. This is an important step to take because it teaches us how to adjust our habits to be more practical and more comfortable to follow.

To analyze this in more depth, we will now examine a recent Princeton study titled "The Good Samaritan." A good Samaritan situation is when someone helps a stranger in need. Students at the divinity school at Princeton decided to put this situation to the test in the real world by administering the following study.

This study featured people who thought that they were about to give presentations on helping those in need. An actor was placed in the hallway towards the stage on which they were going to give their performances. This actor was set on the ground and was made to act like he was in pain and needed help. The participants, however, had been told before that they needed to hurry to get to the presentations, so none of them stopped to help the person in need on their way to give presentations on helping people in need.

The point of this study was to highlight the importance of systems vs. goals. The participants here were goal-oriented. They were there to give presentations, but they let their end-goals cloud their judgments on their ways of meeting this goal. It is never that the goals you set forth are the most essential part of the actions that you are taking—the most crucial part of what you do is always the system that you set forth for doing so.

While it is always important to begin doing whatever it is that you do with an end goal in mind to keep you grounded, on task, and involved in what you are doing—it is much more important that you are sticking to your repetitions of the functions that you are taking up. This will allow you to meet further goals in the future, not just the ones that you are taking up at the moment. Success is always more a matter of growth than of achievement.

The next thing that we should discuss is just how long it takes to meet individual goals. Habits typically take anywhere from 3 weeks to 8 months to become firmly developed. It is more of a lifestyle that you are aiming to establish when you are developing new habits, so once your new habits are developed, and you start to see results you cannot afford to just default to giving up and neglecting to further your progress. This is a conservative attitude to take, and it will invariably lead you back into the same old destructive habits that you started out with. Avoid all of this by staying on top of your development even after you have passed through your initial phase transition into more successful habits.

The power of repetition is not to be underestimated when considering the automaticity of a particular habit. Studies have shown that the more repetitions of something that you do, the more automatic that habit will become for you. At a certain point, however, the habit will become intuitive to you. While practicing beyond that point is still beneficial and even necessary, your skill at that point is already firmly established, and you will have a much easier time doing whatever it is that you have been practicing.

One method of more effective habit formation is what is known as the "three R's" of habit formation these are as follows:

Reminder: This is what initiates the habit. It is, in other words, your cue. For example, you could set the alarm on your phone which tells you to read for 30 minutes every day. This would be your reminder.

Routine: This is the actual act of practicing the habit itself. For example, if you are trying to get in shape going to the gym every day would be your routine for doing so.

## Stephen Patterson

Reward: This is what you get in exchange for the behavior. This can be the most effective way of ensuring that you stick to good habits. Without this step, there is not a visible short-term reward for what you are doing, so you drive to do so will most likely lessen with time. For example, you could reward yourself for reading for 30 minutes by then watching TV for an additional 30 minutes. This will keep you practicing that habit for longer than you would otherwise.

We should now take a look at some of the most reliable methods of sticking to the habits that you set forth for yourself.

The first method for doing this is to keep what you are doing simple. When you first start off employing a habit, you are going to be met with more difficulty if you follow the habit big and complicated. To avoid fatiguing yourself unnecessarily, you should take these three steps: 1. Start off with a habit that you find easy 2. Increase the amount of time and effort that you build into the habit, but by incremental steps and 3. Break the habit down into smaller, more digestible chunks as needed.

These methods all seem very simple and easy to follow in theory, but they prove to be too hard for some to support in practice. Everyone wants to write their own best-selling novel, but very few people are willing to sit down and take the time to write a couple dozen short stories first. It is always more important to stick to your routines rather than to get the results that you are aiming for.

The amount of motivation it takes to start off on developing a habit is always much, much more than it takes to sustain a habit. In fact, it really makes no motivation at all to support a habit. All that you have to do is just keep doing what you are already doing. For example, after running a mile in one direction, it is much easier to run another mile in the other direction to get back home. This is because you are already prepared to do so, and you know that you really have nothing to lose in doing so.

You can also accumulate the positive effects of your habits by setting up your environment in a way that is conducive to making positive gains. You should make it easier to do the things that are good for you and make it harder to do the things that are bad for you. This will make you much more likely to stick to good habits and avoid bad ones. Your goal here is to make making good decisions so easy that you just cannot say no to them.

These cues that we place in front of ourselves are what are known as triggers. Of triggers, there are two types: cold triggers and hot triggers. Hot triggers are things that could be acted upon in the present moment, while cold triggers cannot. For example, a crisp trigger would be a coupon to a restaurant that is going to open up a month from now, while a hot trigger would be a coupon to one that is already open.

Needless to say, it is hot triggers that most people find more appealing. If you want to motivate yourself or others to do something, it is always best to look for hot triggers to do so. Very few people enjoy having to think ahead and following long-term courses of action. Providing hot triggers makes benefits an immediate happening and therefore encourages operations to be performed more.

Of hot and cold triggers five factors go into them, the first of these is time. For example, let's say you have to meet deadlines for projects at work every week. If you have to turn in an invoice every Monday and every Thursday, then it is time which is the main factor driving these actions.

The second factor that affects triggers is location. For example, let's say you go to a gym every day where you do squats using a bar. In this example, it would be the location of the gym which would drive that habit. Another critical factor that affects triggers are the previous events that triggers have. These are events that cue you to perform a habit. For example, if you pray before every meal, then sitting down at the table would be the last event for prayer and prayer would be the previous event for eating.

The fourth factor that affects triggers is your emotional state. The mood that you find yourself intends to have a much more significant impact on your behavior than you might expect. For example, if you come into work in a frustrated mood, you will be much more likely to yell at a coworker if you find yourself getting into a disagreement with one. The fifth and final factor that affects triggers is other people. This factor is a very dynamic one because other people can have a vast variety of effects on our triggers. For example, if you associate yourself with people with anger issues, you are much more likely to develop anger issues yourself.

To find some of the possible triggers that you can then apply other more appropriate triggers too, you should make two lists: the first one being a list of things that you do throughout a day. Go from your morning routine to your midday routine and finally to your nightly routine and examine all of the things that you actively do throughout a day. The next list you should make is one of the things that happen to you throughout a day. These are things that are beyond your control and that you have no say over. Once you have these two lists, you will then have a good indication of all the things that might trigger you throughout a day.

If you do what is listed above and find that some of your reactions to things that happen are not very effective, you should try adjusting those reactions. Doing this will help you remain adaptable because your neuronal connections are already formed for dealing with these triggers, so now you just have to deal with the matter of adjusting your reactions, which is much easier than is experiencing entire new things. In doing this, you are going to tie your new behaviors to the same neural pathways, which will make these much more likely to stick in the long run.

Now that we have a better overview of habits in general, we should take a look at how to know what it is that you need to change and what it is that you do not.

The first step in determining what it is that you need to change in your life is deciding what it is that is distracting you from reaching your goals. One effect that we should go over here is known as the Zeigarnik effect. This is the tendency of people only to remember what is useful to them in the short term. Once you have no more immediate need for the information at hand, however, you then tend just to throw out all of the information that you just spent all of that time learning. This is a great strategy to use in the short term to achieve your goals, but it is not something that will benefit you in the long run.

When you do nothing but let your curiosity get the best of you and absorb whatever information you want to aimlessly you create large loops of more or less useless information that take up lots of your energy and leave about where you started off in the first place. Absorbing and memorizing all of these random pieces of information not only does not get you very far, but it also opens up large nagging gaps in your cognitive energy which divert much-needed energy which could otherwise be used to complete the tasks that you need to achieve in the present moment.

While working hard and multitasking are incredibly important aspects of success you should try to avoid working very much harder than need be, especially on tacks that do not directly benefit you at least in the short term. Doing so will burn out all of your fuel before you can get to the meat of what you really need to do. You may be able to do both your job and all of these other things effectively at first, but after a while, you are bound to wear yourself out if you are continually being split between all of these unnecessary things which you do not really need to do and which do not always help you out.

Another thing that excessive multitasking will deplete is your reserves of willpower. When you are always being divided among multiple elements, the likelihood that you are going to turn down lots of further opportunities is good. You have to keep in mind that no matter who you are there is only so much of you.

One way to deal with situations in which you have to multitask is to prioritize your concerns. To go after all of the things that you have to do each day all at once is to attack a full-fledged hydra. It will overwhelm you, and you will not make as much progress as you would have you just started by picking the situation apart piece by piece.

Your willpower tends to peak during the morning hours, there is then a dip in willpower right before lunch, followed by another spike in willpower right after lunch. One of the keys to having the most auspicious days possible is to ride these waves of willpower for all that they are worth, keeping in mind that they are fleeting and that they are something to be grateful for when they come.

The next step in our effort to better prioritize our efforts to ascertain what exactly it is that we should be prioritizing.

When prioritizing what you need to do with your time, it is the things that are good but not great that you need to avoid doing at all costs. These things should be avoided even more than the things that you do not enjoy doing because you will always lose track of how often you are doing these things. These are where we get into the nagging loops that we find ourselves in, and we usually have trouble getting ourselves out of these. It is a problem of plenty, not of poverty. If you were to make a list of your 25 top priorities, it would be numbered 6-25 that need to be avoided more so than any other things that you do. Again, to take all of these up for yourself would be to try in vain to slay a hydra. Remember, there is only so much of you.

Take growing a rose bush for example. If you want a rose bush to be healthy and to look good, you are going to have to prune some of the bulbs away. There is just no way around this. You cannot expect each and every lamp of a rosebush to look good. Likewise, you cannot plan for each and every one of your interests to be a good use of your time pursuing.

One tool that will help you tell whether or not you should spend your time on something is what is known as the Eisenhower box. In this bow, there are four quadrants. In the upper left quadrant, there are the things that are both important and urgent. In the upper right quadrant, there are the things that are unimportant and urgent. In the lower left quadrant, some things are important and not urgent. Finally, in the lower right quadrant, there are the things that are both unimportant and not urgent. The important things should be delved into first, especially the important things which are also critical. The trivial stuff comes second, though the unimportant things that are also not urgent should be deleted if at all possible.

That concludes our discussion on the accumulation of habits. If you keep looking into the habits that you have in your everyday life and finding things that are not helping you, then you are bound to form new and better habits which will help you achieve more of your goals in the future. The principles laid out within this chapter should give you a good starting off point for doing so.

**Successful Habits of Extraordinary People**

# Chapter 4:
# Keystone Habits and Taking Action

While all of your habits, from the most minuscule to the most important, determine your overall success and well being, there are a few habits that are more seminal to your growth than are any others. These habits are what are known as keystone habits. We should take the opportunity to touch on these habits and delve into what makes them so valuable.

Keystone habits are notable not only in the sense that they are the most important habits we develop but also in the sense that all of our other habits are connected and often dependent on them. For example, let's say that you work out every day. After working out, you will experience a series of changes that will affect the rest of your day. For instance, your focus will almost immediately improve and stay sharper for some time afterward. This will cause at least an hour of much intense focus for you, which will enable you to get more work done quicker and more reliably. The second change that you will notice is that you will eat better without even really thinking about it. Your body tells your mind to provide it with more nutrients when it is put under the extra demands the working out has to give. The third and final effect of working out that you will notice is that you will sleep better. Your mind and body will eventually become fatigued from the excess work that they have done, and you will be able to get to sleep quicker and sleep longer.

Working out is just one of many examples of keystone habits employed by the most successful among us. Others include meditation, going on daily walks, afternoon naps, etc. These and many others are continuously used by successful people to keep them running at their top capacity, and once these habits have been developed, they tend to trickle into every other facet of life. This can usually create positive self-reinforcing loops, which can build upon themselves and create a completely different experience for the person feeding the positive habit—though negative habits also have this tendency to metastasize throughout the rest of a person's life.

Hence, as you can see by now, keystone habits will have wide-ranging effects on the rest of your life, which can do a lot to help you with virtually everything else that you do throughout any given day. The next topic that we should discuss now is how to take action when it comes to employing new and better habits.

### Stephen Patterson

The first step to taking action in regards to your new habits is called pre-commitment. Pre-commitment works on the notion that willpower can be depleted and that when our willpower is low, we tend to give up lots of our goals and habits. We also are less inclined to make choices in general when we do not have that much willpower. Whereas we usually are caught up among too many decisions to be able to make any effect, when we are depleted of willpower, we cannot make choices at all.

When you do this to a specific action or behavior, you decrease your likelihood of not following through with the activity or behavior when the chosen time allotment comes up. For example, if you decide to fill out a survey at 6 P.M. one day rather than just trying to do it at some random time, then you are going to be much more likely to stick to your plan and get the survey over with.

One of the most effective methods of ensuring that you are following through with the goals that you set forth for yourself is what is known as implementation assurance. This involves providing that you stick to a schedule of practice by first writing down the time and place that you are going to perform the action at. This will give you a solid reminder of what you need to do to progress and when to do so. People who write down when and where they are going to perform a task are, on average, around 50% more likely to stick to that task. It is much easier to stick to doing something once you have made something of a contract with yourself that you are in fact going to do that thing at x place and at y time.

Now that we have established a suitable method of starting a new behavior out by writing down when and where we are going to perform the task, we should get into how to stick to the new routine in the long run and how to continue to improve on it moving forward.

One method that is useful for establishing habits, in the long run, is what is known as the paperclip method. This method involves putting a set number of paperclips in a jar and moving them over to another jar every time you complete a task. For example, let's say you work in telemarketing and you have 120 paperclips in your jar. You could move one of these over each and every time that you make a sales call in a year, and by the end of the year, you would be a much more successful worker. This goes to show that no matter what it is that you do, there are usually one or two fundamental tasks involved in the work on which everything else is dependent. These are your keystone habits that determine the success of your entire enterprise, so practicing these and increasing the frequency at which you perform these tasks will help you more than working on other tasks.

## Stephen Patterson

Another beneficial factor of this technique is the visual cue that it provides. You are always in sight of all that you have achieved so far as well as how far you have to go to meet your goal when using this strategy. You can see all of the paperclips clearly when doing this. This makes you more immediately aware of where you are at right now, which differs from the norm, where we cannot tell where we are precisely on a particular task.

To further explore how the environment can shape our behaviors, we will now take a look at a study carried out at Harvard to determine whether or not we can influence people's habits and behaviors without even talking to anyone. This was, of course, all done through manipulating the environment around the test subjects.

They used the cafeteria at Massachusetts General Hospital as their environment. As far as drinks were concerned, they placed water fountains around the cafeteria as well as refrigerators that had both water and soda in them. In one case they still included soda in the fridges, but they added more bottles of water than before. What they found, in this case, is that people were much more inclined to but water under these circumstances. In fact, water sales increased by 26%, and soda sales decreased by 16%.

# Successful Habits of Extraordinary People

This shows that 16% of the people who originally bought soda only did so because that was what was put in front of them. We can infer from this that a lot of the decisions that we make in everyday life are more based on what is in our immediate environment rather than what we think we want.

This study goes to show the importance of tailoring your own environment to make things that are bad for you harder to obtain so that all of your lazy, default decisions will be good ones. If, for example, your popcorn is placed on the top shelf of your cabinet where it requires a step stool to get to it, while your apples are placed at arm's reach, then you are going to be much more likely to eat apples of the two choices.

As you can see now, a person's behavior is significant—if not solely—influenced by his or her environment. With that being said, it is nearly impossible to achieve all of the things that you want to accomplish if you are stuck in a negative situation and are making no attempts to escape it.

Another key to taking action is, again, persistence. Let's say that you want to write better jokes. The only reliable way of doing this would be to get and stay in the habit of writing jokes each and every day. Get a whiteboard calendar and mark off every day that you write a joke with an X if you have to. If you keep doing it every day then you will start to get longer, and longer chains of X's going, it is then that you will begin to see improvement in the quality of your jokes.

There are, of course, going to be days in which you break these chains and neglect to work on whatever it is that you work on. This mental model that you should observe under these circumstances is "never miss twice." It is not that the most successful people never make mistakes and or neglect their responsibilities, the only difference here between the successful and the unsuccessful is the fact that the successful do not get into the habit of ignoring their responsibilities in the long term.

There is a zone of long-term growth that we should also touch on now. This zone is somewhere in between complete laziness and complete burnout and here is where you should stay if you want to be successful in the long term. Success is, as are all other things, all about balance, so you cannot expect to work yourself too hard or do not work at all and still get forward in life.

Next, we need to clarify one concept that is all too often reversed in the minds of most people—motivation stems from the action and not the other way around. In other words, inspiration does not come to the lazy.

## Successful Habits of Extraordinary People

It is almost never the case that any of the great composers, for example, popped out of their beds in the morning with brilliant new ideas for their symphonies, string quartets, etc., as Hollywood would like to have you believe. All of their greatest works were, instead, usually brought about by long and tireless hours spent at their desks with their manuscript papers below their hands. If you want to get good ideas and to produce good things, you are going first to have to sit down and think what you want to produce out for yourself.

Again, you have to be selective about what you choose to spend your time doing. Here are some excellent questions to ask yourself before scheduling out time to focus on a specific task:

- What is the main reason that I have for completing this task?

- What am I going to feel like once I am done with it?

- Will this improve my life, and if so, how?

Asking yourself these questions and others like them will help you filter out any of the tasks that you do not need to perform. When stepping back and looking objectively at your reasons for completing a mission, you will get a better understanding of just how essential and or urgent the task at hand is. You can now refer back to the Eisenhower box mentioned in chapter three if you need to.

Once you have determined that a task is worth your time, you should then start to formulate a plan as to how you are going to about completing that task. This could be formatted something like this: Desired Goal - Positive Change - Clear Plan - Committed Action - Desired Outcome.

The desired goal here is clear. This is whatever you want to achieve. The positive change here would be where all of the microhabitat strategies laid out earlier would come into play. This is probably the single most crucial part of the whole plan as it is here that the tools that you use to meet all of your future goals are gained. The next step here is having a clear idea. This one is difficult because plans have the annoying tendency to meander with the change of circumstances that accompany them. In other words, what might seem like a definite plan one day is bound to be a bit different the next day. Ideas can be fickle, so it is essential to keep a few select desired outcomes in mind when progressing in your habits in the future. This will make your plans for meeting these goals much clearer. The next step that we have here is the step of committed action. This is where persistence starts to play a significant role. Again, the goal in this step is to start off chains of practice each and every day and never to miss more than two days in a row. Finally, we come to the last step, the desired outcome. This is, in other words, the fruits of our labor. If the desired result is never met, which it usually is, then it may be helpful to go back and reanalyze the way in which you went about achieving your goal.

We now need to consider two of the most common things that prevent people from ever reaching their goals. These two things are 1. A lack of self-discipline which prevents people from staying persistent in their goals and 2. A scarcity of self-efficacy which causes people to lack faith in themselves and their ability to achieve their goals.

The former of these two disadvantages are usually very clear to see by all. The latter, on the other hand, is often more concealed and harder to detect in people.

Of these two we should first discuss self-discipline. This is something that most of the entire world lacks. If you were to give the average person you meet on the street $80,000 per year for nothing there is an excellent chance that that person will not wind up producing anything of any value. This is because people just do not like to work, especially not if they see no immediate and direct benefit from working. With this being said it becomes clear that you need to continually remind yourself when working on something that what you are doing is going to be worthwhile. Otherwise, you have no incentive to continue working on the task.

The two main pillars of self-discipline are time management and persistence. When you allow yourself to waste time with trivialities and unnecessary things you are welcoming all sorts of destructive habits in their wake. You need to remain focused on the goal at hand when you are working, that way you will keep bad habits at bay and continue to build productive habits which will help you meet all of your future goals. If you remain focused on the one task that you are assigned with at any given moment, you will also gain more energy and perseverance in doing so because your mind will not be split up among all of these other factors that you do not need to be focusing on. This harkens back to the points made on nagging loops of arbitrary efforts brought up in previous chapters. By zooming in on one particular task, you can give the work more of your attention.

If you do not want to lead a mediocre life, which you do not if you are reading this book, then you are going to have to remain aware of all of the tasks that you are presented with which do not offer you much advantage and which you would be better off not focusing on. To be successful it is not just necessary to know what you want, but also to understand what you do not want.

The next trait that we should spend some time discussing is self-efficacy. Self-efficacy is the strength of belief that you have in your own abilities. When you have low self-efficacy, you tend to underestimate your own ability to meet your goals, which often makes you less likely to even start out on new projects. This makes you far less productive than you would otherwise be and it prevents you from ever moving forward in life.

Having low self-efficacy has a wide variety of effects on your entire life. Low self-efficacy often makes people hesitant to try out new things due to fear of failure, which then leads to people not leading their lives as fully as they would otherwise. If you have low self-efficacy just remember before producing anything that your only job is to put whatever it is that you make out there. Believe in what you do and put your products out there, then all you can do is let the world decide what it likes best.

People who have high self-efficacy, on the other hand, tend to approach more demanding tasks with more confidence. This often leads them into more and better opportunities and more fulfilling lives overall. People with low self-efficacy are more likely to avoid challenges and to give up on meeting or never try to meet their goals. They also more often than not believe more than any sort of change is not possible or too hard to achieve. If you want to rid yourself of self-doubt and raise your levels of self-efficacy, as well as meet any goals that you have in mind, you should try to follow the steps mentioned below:

- Identify a reason for meeting the goal
- Determine that the desired outcome is, in fact, a positive change
- Develop your self-discipline every day
- Manage your time effectively and prioritize what it is that you work on
- Recognize that your limiting beliefs are slowing you down and work on adjusting them
- Stay persistent
- Reward yourself for keeping on track in whatever it is that you do
- Repeat

So, to conclude, keystone habits are the habits which determine so much of what your life consists of surrounding these habits. To take action and to start pursuing your goals requires the adjustment of your environment, persistence in whatever it is that you do, and pre-commitment to your habits, whatever they might be, among other things. Following these procedures in going about your daily work will help you organize your production and make progress faster and more effectively.

# Chapter 5:
# The Secret Habits of the Successful

When most people think of success, they think of lots of money and luxury items and having a high-paying job. This is, however, a grossly misguided concept of what being successful is. While everyone has their own personal version of what constitutes success, most versions have a few things in common—among these are job satisfaction and access to the same opportunities that everyone else has. This might sound like a platitude, but it is true nonetheless: it is far more important than your heart and soul are involved in what you do than it is that you make lots of money from. If you only get money out of what you do, then that is all that you are going to be left with. Conversely, if you just get satisfaction out of an activity, then that is all that you are going to receive.

The main things that are holding us back in most of the endeavors that we take up are usually not the things that we expect. Instead, it is often our own misperceptions about ourselves that discourage us from moving forward by any larger degrees. This goes back to the facts pointed out on the topic of low self-efficacy in the last chapter; frequently, we hold ourselves back from trying new things due to self-imposed borders that we create. This, in turn, leads us to live less involved lives than we sometimes deserve.

As you have already heard, our realities are only what we perceive them to be. With this said, it would then follow that if you recognize your truth to be a bad and unwelcoming one than you are less likely to move on to better realities. You can move forward and continue to grow and change while still being satisfied with what you have at the present moment. If you make your own personal reality out to be a hellish landscape, then it will most likely become that way. Here, as anywhere, the power of positivity takes precedence over that of cynicism or even "realism." While it is important to stay grounded, all too many modern attitudes are marked by a shallow sophistication that prides itself on pessimism and cynicism.

As Hobbes once famously pointed out, civilization cannot exist without suffering. If everyone were to get whatever they wanted automatically, there would cease to be civilization itself. When you see someone who you want to emulate or something that you want to own, it is not always easy to know the pain that was required to obtain that person's status or the labor that went into producing that thing. It is this pain and this labor, however, which are the only things that make these things worthwhile. If there is never anything put into achieving something, then there will never be anything to be gotten out of it—it has no worth if no worth has been put into it.

It is this pain that is poured into the fruits of your labor that not only makes what you worthwhile but also gives you something to work to avoid. Pain can serve as a weight that you can pull against to meet your goals. Take the immigrants from third world countries who come to America and become doctors for example. These people end up accomplishing more than most born Americans because, in part, they have things to avoid in their home countries. They have seen more poverty and despair than any of the rest of us have seen, so they know that they need to work extra hard to avoid living like that again.

There are always going to be periods in your life which will shake you to your foundations. It is in these periods that all of the negative things that people tell you are going to come back to bother you to their full extent, which you need to use to your advantage here. This is why it is always so important to cut out the negative people in your life. Over the years of being around negative people, the/ negative beliefs that they will instill in you will accumulate over time and sometimes this all will boil over into you losing some of your self-efficacy. It is during these periods that your real character is going to be tested because it sometimes takes lots of strength to stick to your goals during these periods of high stress and self-doubt. Under these circumstances, you must stay persistent in whatever it is that you do and curtail self-doubt and worry as much as possible.

It is after these periods of great adversity, usually, that The Grapes of Wrath start to show themselves. It is typically true that the bigger the hits you sustain, the bigger the payoff will be for your having done so. The great gift in adversity is always the grit and the fear that it instills in us. Without any difficulty, a person becomes spoiled, lazy, and often entitled. And even after adversity, the only way to curtail some of the more self-indulgent personality traits is to continually remind yourself of some of the adverse effects of your giving up.

Here the saying runs as accurate as ever: if you upgrade your success, you enhance your problems. After we find ourselves on the other end of hard times, it is always important to remind ourselves that we are capable of getting through basically anything that is put in front of us. We should, however, still expect to be beset on all sides by adversity in whatever it is that we do and wherever it is that we go. Increasing on what it is that you do will not decrease your amount of suffering, in fact, it is ultimately only going to expand it. You may ask yourself the question under these circumstances: why is it worth it in that case? To that one answer may be that you may find that there are things that offset the cost of suffering along the path to your success. It is only by realizing this that you can turn the hardest periods in your life into the best and most productive ones. If you are using your own suffering as that source of your inspiration, then you are going to find yourself with an endless supply of inspiration, because the adversity that you face is always going to be constant.

Another very crucial factor that goes into success is confidence. We need to be continually protecting our own confidence levels throughout each and every day to make the best decisions possible and to move forward in whatever it is that we do. When you think back on all of the significant decisions that you had made recently when your confidence was low, odds are that they turned out to be less effective than the ones that you created when your confidence was high. This is because you usually make more passive, defensive, and rapport seeking decisions when your faith is low. You cannot discern your own constructive attributes, which makes you underestimate your own decision-making abilities, which in turn makes your decision making even worse. This can create an endless cycle of low confidence followed by a decrease in decision-making ability and so on and so forth.

## Successful Habits of Extraordinary People

Now we should discuss habit formation in everyday life in greater detail. The first thing that you get to every day is obviously your morning routine, so this routine and its effectiveness can make or break the success of your entire day. One of the greatest things that you can do in the morning which is shared by all of the most successful people in the world is listing the things that you are grateful for. This will not only give you a better perspective on all of the great things that you already have, but it is also scientifically proven to be the quickest way of improving your mood at any given time. Each day when you wake up one of your first priorities should not be to get to work or finish a side project, but instead, it should be to make a brief list of all of the things that you are grateful for. Let's say that you do this for two weeks. Most of us would run out of things to list within that time period. After you have run out of things that you can list you should then look for more things that you missed the first time around. If you keep trying to fill the list with more and more things that you had not noticed initially you are bound to come up with ideas that you would never have seen otherwise. If you continue this strategy for a year you are going to end up with an entirely new perspective on life at the year's end.

Another excellent morning routine to adopt is recalling the good things that happened the previous day and thinking of what good things could happen today or what you need to get done throughout the day. These practices will both keep you grateful for the things that you have been given recently and keep you on your toes as to what you need to do next. One more great thing to do in the morning is running through some of the personal affirmation that you like best. This is a great way to change your vibrational frequency as far as attitude is concerned and to adjust whatever may some of the faultier attitudes in place within your subconscious be. Often times attitudes get placed into us so far down that we can find it hard to dislodge them. Affirmations are a great way to adjust these sometimes very pesky attitudes, especially if they are done throughout a prolonged period of time. When repeating affirmations to yourself, there are two things to keep in mind if you want to do so more effectively. One is to visualize what it is that you are saying to yourself. This will give you a mental image of what you are going for which will cement the idea into your mind much more effectively. The second thing is to formulate and maintain a clear concept of what it is that you are going for. The more you repeat our affirmations, the more real they will become. If you stick to saying just one or two things over and over again to yourself day in and day out, you are bound to see lots of results in your attitudes and how you think in your future. Some of the greatest affirmations for success are as follows: "I excel in all that I do, and success comes easily to me." "I am constantly presented with new opportunities and successes," and "I always dress for success in body, mind, and spirit." Again, if you repeat these affirmations to yourself and keep repeating them, then they will only become more and more accurate for you.

Your morning routine should then be punctuated by the quotidian tasks that you have to take upon yourself every day. After that, we move into your brunch/ midday routine. This is where most people go on meal breaks and or go to the gym. Be careful not to spend too much time on leisure throughout these hours because there is still a lot of work that you need to do for the day around this time and it is also around this time that you start to get your daily peaks in libido, energy levels, and even logical reasoning. It is throughout this part of the day that you should use any and all downtime that you may get to analyze and improve on the habits that you exhibited throughout the morning hours. This will help you set more effective goals pertaining to the rest of your day. The hours around noon are also when you are probably going to communicate with the most substantial amount of people throughout the day. It would follow that you should probably use this time to say anything that is on your mind to those around you. Just keep in mind while doing this that you still have nearly half of the day to go through so you may want to be careful about what you say as far as criticisms or confrontations are concerned.

Next, you will find yourself entering the afternoon hours. This is the homestretch of the workday, and your performance here has a direct impact on what your workload will be the next day. This only important thing to keep in mind about working throughout these hours is that you need to stay persistent in what it is that you do here. It is all too easy to let yourself get tired and start falling behind during these hours, which is a mistake that very many, if not most, people make that holds them back significantly in the long run if they keep to these annoying habits that cause this dip in productivity after lunch.

It is throughout the afternoon hours that your reaction times are at their fastest, your blood pressure peaks (which, by the way, some potassium at lunch will help curtail), and your muscle strength is at its highest. Your cortisol (a mood stabilizer) levels are also at their highest throughout the afternoon hours, which will make you think more rationally and keep you from having any drastic mood swings. It should also be noted that people are much more likely to rush what they are doing throughout these hours and therefore more mistakes are made on everyday tasks throughout these hours.

Finally, we reach the evening hours. One of your main goals on any given day is to finish all of your daily tasks before these hours so that you will be able to finish off the day with some downtime. It is during this time that we can relax and enjoy the rewards of the efforts that we made throughout the day. If you go into the evening hours with lots of work still to do, then you are not going to enjoy your time because you will have to spend it all doing things that you have to do rather than what to do.

While the evening is the best time to relax and be lazy, it would still be beneficial for you to use this time to get ahead in regards to the tasks that you have yet to do. Doing this will keep you ahead of many because not a lot of people do this with their time. All too many people out there just punch in their eight or so hours and then put little to no thought into how they are going to spend the rest of the hours in the day. Let's say you work from 9 - 5. If you go to bed around 10 each night, then you have within this schedule the time slot of 5 - 10 completely open. This is where the average person watches TV, eats, and may converse with others. If you take this time and divide hour by hour, you will start to see a lot of opportunities that you may be missing out on in regards to developing your skills and pursuing your passions with more intensity.

## Stephen Patterson

It is typically the evening hours in which we finally get time throughout the day to do whatever it is that we want to do. The key then to using these hours to our advantage would be to define better what it is that we want to do the most. If you are just spending these hours jumping randomly from one fancy to the next, then you are bound to make no progress in anything you do. In this case, you will live like peter pan in Neverland. You will be suffocated by your own pleasures, which will not only grow old in no time at all but will also never allow you to grow in any way.

Throughout your entire day, one of the main things that you can do to be more productive is to schedule out your time. If you are not considering time than you are ignoring an entire dimension. It should be noted that you can schedule your time in any way that you like, but you are going to have to be wise about the amount of time that you devote to certain things. If, for instance, you schedule out 2 hours each third day of your life for laser tag, then you can expect to get much better at playing laser tag, but you cannot expect to learn differential calculus this way.

The secret habits of the most successful are not so esoteric as some would like for you to believe. They are, on the whole, based on common sense and are very easy and straightforward to apply to your everyday life. Remember here that success is a lifestyle. It is not just one or two choices that you make once or twice, it is the way in which you conduct yourself day in and day out. If you want to achieve long-term success in whatever it is that you do, you are going to have to make long-term adjustments in your habits and your attitudes.

# Chapter 6:
# Keys to Financial Success

In this chapter, we should discuss ways to manage your finances successfully. This is one area in which most people strive for success more so than in other areas. In determining how to achieve financial success, we need first to define what financial success could mean.

When we think of financial success, some of the images that come to mind can be deceiving. The word may conjure up images of luxury items and fancy foods in our minds, but financial success is more about things like security, physical comfort, free time, and peace of mind surrounding your finances. You can use the money that you earn more effectively by investing in your safety in case of any calamities you might face in the future, better food and better means of making yourself comfortable. Earning more money in less time so that you have more time to spend doing the things that you love, and having the assurance that you are prepared for anything else that might set your path in the future.

One may, and maybe the best way, to better gauge your own financial success is to keep track of the financial milestones that you come across. These could include things like paying off your first home, paying your college tuition off in full, paying off a car, and getting out of debt for good.

Before getting into tips regarding financial success, it should be mentioned that these by no means ensure that you are going to make more money in the future. These will, however, provide useful blueprints for your search on success. Some of the most excellent tips regarding finances that you may ever receive are listed below:

**Make Sure to Spend Less Money Than You Earn.**
This tip can be surprisingly hard to implement, especially when you find yourself in situations in which you are struggling and living paycheck to paycheck. This is especially unfortunate because this is one of the most essential tips that will be listed here regarding your financial success. When deciding what you should spend your money on, you should not underestimate the importance of differentiating between the things that you want and the things that you need. For example, a reliable vehicle may be a need for you depending on where you live, but a luxury car with all the works is always going to be a want and a wantonly. This

is where all of the advertisements and sponsored content that we come into contact with on a daily basis can prove to do us a lot of harm. We are often convinced to buy things that we do not need and hardly even want without us realizing it because we are overexposed continuously to these forms of content.

Instead of buying whatever it may be that other people who do not have your best interests in mind tell you to buy on a whim, buy, at first, only the essentials that sustain yourself day in and day out. These often include things like food, toiletries, and shelter. It is only once all of these things have been accounted for that you can start spending your money on the things that you want.

## Trust Your Instincts.

You cannot expect anyone else to have your own interests in mind to the same degree that you do. This is why you should always err on the side of excessive caution when it comes to making deals and or agreements with others on financial matters. You are ultimately going to be held responsible for all and any of the decisions that you make regarding your finances, so if a particular decision does not feel right to you, then you should probably avoid making it.

## Fulfill the Responsibilities That You Have to Loved Ones.

Here we should discuss some essential types of insurance in case anything happens to you. You have to remember when financing that you are not the only person who is going to be affected if something wrong happens to you. The three most important types of insurance that you can purchase for the well-being of your loved ones are as follows:

*Health insurance.* There is an extremely high likelihood that you are going to develop some sort of medical condition or illness in your future that is going to require treatment. The costs for medical procedures, especially in the US, is very high, as you already know, so health insurance is a must despite how healthy you may be. Unless you are self-employed, one of the most effective methods of saving money on a plan is to go through your employer's system. You should also look for higher deductibles if you want to pay less for monthly premiums. Most average earning workers would be wise to look for higher deductibles than they typically do because odds are that you are not going to spend all that much on health care costs annually if you are in good health. Looking into whether or not you qualify for a health savings account (HSA) is also beneficial in your cutting down on insurance costs. This may be the most crucial form of insurance that is going to be listed here because it is usually the most immediately applicable in most people's lives.

*Life insurance.* If you are a young and single person then life insurance is typically going to be much more affordable because you only need to pay for your own funeral service and your casket. Older people with children, on the other hand, have to buy a plan that is going to provide their families with income beyond their deaths. These plans usually support their kids until they become adults or until they graduate from college. In the average middle-class family, the cost of raising a child to their age of 18 is around $227,000. If the child then decides to go to college, the price for doing so will be approximately $17,000 per year for tuition, room, and board. For a private four-year college, this rate is even higher at around $32,000 a year. The cost of life insurance for a young adult, however, is somewhat inexpensive. In fact, the average nonsmoker below the age of 25 can usually get a plan with payments of $25 per month for $500,000 worth of life insurance. If you are a parent with a spouse, then you should ensure that both of you have insurance plans. This will keep your children supported in case both of you die before the children reach adulthood.

*Disability insurance.* The odds of suffering an injury that keeps you from working for 90 days within a year are %80 for the average 25-year-old. Your own odds may be higher or lower depending on your work and your lifestyle, but on the whole, it is always beneficial to consider a disability insurance package. Do not let the fact that you are healthy right now deter you from getting this insurance. It can be astonishing just how quickly a person can go from being in good health to being disabled. Some may not realize this, but most employers offer disability insurance packages in addition to health insurance packages. Looking into these could provide you with peace of mind that you would not have otherwise.

You are always going to have responsibilities to fulfill for your loved ones, so the sooner that you start focusing on how you are going to help them out in the event of some calamity or another the better. This is especially true if you have any dependents. These people cannot afford to live without your continued support, so you are obligated to plan ahead for them in case anything terrible happens to you.

### Keep and Protect an Emergency Cash Fund.

As a general rule of thumb, the amount of money that you have in your emergency fund should be equivalent to six months of your average income. For example, if you make $50,000 a year, then your emergency fund should have $25,000 in it at all times. Bad things can pop out of the blue at any time, and often when we expect them to the least. This amount needs to be met before you consider making any long-term investments in anything else. To strategize the other way around would be to build a house on foundations of sand. While this rate of six months' income may seem needlessly high, the average time span between jobs is around seven months, so this emergency fund may not even last you the entire time period in which you are in between jobs.

One quick way to build emergency funds up offered by many employers is matching funds plans. These are company sponsored plans in which your employer will match dollar for dollar your investment, which will make it a lot easier and quicker to raise the funds you need for emergencies. Besides, these plans ensure that you will make a 100% return on your portion before making any investment earnings. For these reasons you would be wise to take advantage of any of these opportunities whenever they may come along.

Your emergency fund should always be low-risk security, so you should make sure to look into the rates offered by the US treasury bonds and notes, as well as any savings accounts provided by any banks or institutions. Credit unions are one thing, in particular, to look out for, as they will often offer higher interest rates of savings accounts that most banks will.

### Make Good Use of Your Time.

You cannot rely on wishful thinking to bring you any closer to financial success. Keep in mind that the vast majority financial success is a result a lifetime accumulation, not winning the lottery or inheriting an estate. It is time and the consistent management of it that are the keys to long-term financial success.

For example, if you were to save $100 a month from age 25 to age 65 in an account with a 5% interest rate, you would wind up saving $145,000 for retirement. The important thing about saving money is that you are establishing the habit of setting aside some amount of money, no matter how small, every month.

### Diversify Your Investments

Diversifying your investments is the best way to balance your risks vs. your rewards. Once you have obtained adequate insurance and adequate emergency fund, you can then start looking into making other investments. There are innumerable things that you can invest your money in, and each will have their own investment characteristics.

To start off, you may want to stick to more common stocks. These are more popular among beginners because their prices are always available and securities can usually be purchased for them with ease. Equity securities can be bought in multiple ways: as stock in a single company, as stocks in different companies within the same industry, of as stocks in various companies in different sectors. There are also some equity securities that are managed by professional managers who will most likely know more about the industry than you do. Real estate is typically more popular as a place to invest because of the income tax benefits that it offers, but real estate is also usually more expensive to buy and sell than other investments, meaning that it is harder to turn your investment into cash with real estate.

It does not matter what you decide to invest in- markets will always be volatile, meaning that prices will go up and down depending on the number of people purchasing something or another at any given point in time. We remain aware of the fluctuations in the price of stocks from day to day because they are always mentioned in news outlets, but what always flies under our radar are the fluctuations in real estate values. This is just one circumstance under which it becomes helpful to diversify your investments. No more than 10% of your investments should be placed in securities or real estate because their value is just too volatile ever to be a reliable source of income.

## Take the Long Roads When Aiming for Financial Success

There is a term in investing that refers to an investor's willingness to put his or her self-up against uncertain market circumstances called "risk tolerance." A person who has high-risk tolerance is more inclined to take up riskier investments, whereas someone with low-risk understanding is more inclined to take the safer routes to wealth.

On the whole, you should avoid or get rid of investments that give you too much anxiety. If doing so does not prove to be a sound financial decision, then at least you will still gain some peace of mind having the weight of an investment that you did not know about off your chest. There are, after all, way too many great investment opportunities out there to take up any ones that you are not very sure about. The better and safer ones will allow you to meet all of your goals without losing any sleep over the decisions that you are making. If you only make the most reliable choices possible and still find that you are beset by misfortune, then do not panic, instead, find out what your best possible options are moving forward and act on them as quickly as possible. While bad investment returns cannot be redeemed, you can still move on to the next opportunity that presents itself so that you are never entirely ruined. Here again, diversifying your investments will prove to be very beneficial to you.

Stephen Patterson

## Get and Stay Out of Debt.

Debt can metastasize throughout all areas of your life. Once you find yourself in debt you never feel secure and taking any steps forward becomes more or less impossible. So long as you find yourself in debt, you will never be able to fully enjoy any of the things that you come across because you are always behind financially. Avoiding more debt remains essential when you are already in debt. Lots of people make the mistake of thinking that they have so much debt that there is no more in trying to curtail any future deficits. At this point, they give up hope and just continue to waste their money without any plans to manage their financial lives any wiser.

The most effective ways to avoid debt are also the most obvious: avoid excessive spending, and keep track of your payments on everything. Do not spend any money on things that you cannot afford and do not need. One way to make yourself observe this rule is to ask yourself before any purchases: do I need this or do I want this? If the answer is that you only want it, then you should not buy it if you are already in debt. It would also be wise to be wise to limit your number of credit cards because having too many will make you more inclined to spend more on everything. Keeping track of your payments is one aspect of financial success that lots of people (mostly young) have a hard time with. To do this correctly, you should write your payments down on the regular and make sure that you follow through with all of them.

If, on the other hand, you are already in debt than there are also some ways that you can get out of it quickly. The first would be only to make your payments soon so that you do not have to pay as much for APRs. The second way to get out of debt quickly would be to see if you can lower your interest rates. This can sometimes be done by asking your bank or institution to adjust your plan or by transferring your balance to a card with a lower interest rate.

**Establish A Good Credit History.**
Your entire financial reputation is built upon your credit score. With that being said, the merits or demerits of this score can determine your economic life. The easiest way of ensuring that this score is a good one is to make all of your payments on time. Since your credit score is an indication of your overall credit activity, you must be able to keep your credit in order in every one of these areas to maintain a good score.

It takes far more effort to raise your score than to lower it, so take extra care to ensure that you are not getting into any habits of neglecting your payments and or making any of them late. It can be hard to get out of these bad habits once they are created, and you will always be surprised at just how quickly they can ruin your score along with the rest of your financial life.

Success is not all about finances, but being comfortable and secure financially is necessary for your success in any other facets of life. Sticking to the principles laid out in this chapter will help you achieve and maintain financial success in your future. While these habits will most likely never make you rich, they will, however, allow you to live more comfortably if you apply them continuously while making your financial decisions. If you are patient and persistent in taking control of your financial life, then you will start to reap the rewards of doing so quicker than you might expect.

Successful Habits of Extraordinary People

## Chapter 7:
## Keys to Social Success

Every now and then, you come across a person who is so socially well adapted that you find yourself floored. Conversing with these people comes so naturally because of the confidence and fluency of their speech and demeanor. It can almost make you jealous at times to meet these people who have these excellent communication abilities. It is as if these people were chosen to have the world in the palm of their hands because that is precisely how having good communication abilities can feel at times. For those of us who are on the quieter end of the spectrum, it can seem almost impossible to hold oneself to these standards, but there are nevertheless some strategies that you can use to better your conversational abilities.

It is essential to keep a growth mindset rather than a fixed mindset when it comes to communication. It may seem more or less impossible to adjust your level of popularity at will, but you have to keep in mind that even if you have the worst possible reputation, nothing remains set in stone as far as your social skills are concerned. Here, we should take a look at some of the most effective ways to better your interpersonal skills and communication abilities.

## Put More Effort into Showing Interest Than into Being Interesting.

There is a common misconception surrounding popularity that misleads people into thinking that the most famous people among us are the most interesting at all times. This is actually not the case. The main thing that people want to be assured of when they are speaking to others is that they are being listened to and understood by an interested counterpart. This is why it is always much more important to show a genuine interest in what others are saying when they say it. Doing this will make you much more popular than merely having the most exciting things to say.

It should also be noted that people only get bored when others are talking excessively. It does not take nearly as much to lose someone's interest than to gain it. If you drone on excessively about superfluous topics, then people will generally be less inclined to want to talk to you in the future. Giving others the room and time to speak more than yourself will always make them feel more welcomed and more socially desirable themselves. You should also make it a point to call people by their names as much as possible. Doing this will make people feel more connected to you and will project to them that you care about them.

## Remain Positive When Speaking to People—But Not Overly Positive.

There is nothing more exhausting than being around an overly negative person. These people who always expect the worst out of everyone around them and are typically rather outspoken about it will suck the life out of you more quickly than nearly any other force that you will come into contact with. If you ever find yourself in a situation in which you are closer to being one of these people than not, you should make some adjustments to your attitudes and try to project that you are remaining positive. This is not to say that you have to be all sunshine and rainbows nor that you have to be otherwise inauthentic, but you should put some effort into being more positive when talking to other people.

On the whole, excessive negativity is usually much more harmful than excessive positivity, so always err on the side of remaining too positive. Doing this will make you much more desirable to others and will increase your amount of good relationships in the future. You should, however, try to find a balance in doing this to ensure that you can remain somewhat consistent in your demeanor throughout friendship.

## Avoid Gossip Like the Plague That It Is.

Avoid gossip at all costs. While chatter may win you friends and or allegiances in the short term, slandering people behind their backs will always lead you toward negative consequences in the long run. Unless you want others to speak negatively about you behind your back, you should avoid doing so to others. It should also be added that gossiping about others will make those who you do so with less inclined to trust you and divulge any personal information to you because there proves to be a chance of you stabbing them in the back. Gossiping is a petty, superficial, and indirect way to communicate ideas. It does not serve you in the long run and has minimal effect in the short term.

Gossiping is also often a sign of insecurity and weakness. The entire communication strategy is based upon the premise of tearing others down to build yourself up, which is never a good way to deal with any of your problems. If you want to avoid other people sticking their noses into your business, then you should avoid doing the same to others. It is not your business whatever others' problems may be, and you are always better off focusing on how to solve your own problems first. In gossiping, you are also potentially creating victims of your own insecurities who do not deserve the treatment that they are being dealt. If you are solving your own problems, then you have no room for gossip. If you are not addressing your own problems, then you have no right to gossip. In either scenario, gossip has no place in your life.

## Remain Helpful and Dependable

You should offer your assistance when and wherever you can do so with a minimum of inconvenience. We use the phrase "minimum of inconvenience" here because helping people excessively can be even more harmful than never helping anyone at all. All too often overly agreeably people spend their entire lives helping out others out of fear of abandonment among other things and get nothing in return for doing so. Instead, they are stepped all over by all those who they come into contact with and often are never able to break these chains of people who come into their lives and bulldoze over their own self-interests.

This is not to say, however, that you should never help others. Helping others will often benefit you socially. It gives you "points" concerning game theory. It should also be mentioned here the importance of following through on the promises you make. Your reputation can be damaged by unfilled promises even more so than by no promises made at all.

## Serve Your Time as A Matchmaker.

It is often that people will be more drawn to you because of the people who you introduce them to. You should always make it a point to introduce people to others to make yourself more desirable by proxy. You can do this by introducing people to one another one by one, or you can form larger groups when doing things. The more gatherings that you spearhead among people you know, the more you will be perceived as that type of person who can pull people together by others.

Keeping your social network as interconnected as possible will help you forge larger bands of alliances. It will also give you a sense that you are part of something larger than yourself, almost like a community. It is here that you will start to see your number of friends increase because you have more friends in the first place. Your popularity can improve in this way exponentially. You should, however, always keep your manners in mind when out with friends though. This means that you should never neglect an opportunity to introduce a friend to others or vice versa. Ignoring to do this can make you come across as aloof or uncaring, which will make people want to avoid you in the future.

**Maintain Your Self-Awareness.**
You have to be able to step outside of yourself and see your personality in a more objective lens to succeed in anything in life, including making and keeping more friends. This is not to say that you should allow yourself to become overly concerned with what people think of you though. While it is essential to know how people really perceive you it is always more important to maintain some level of self-esteem. You should take

a healthy and moderate amount of stock in what others think of you just out of respect for their opinions if nothing else.

There are many things that you do on a regular basis that you might not even notice. For instance, you may wear a perpetual frown on your face that you are not aware of that other people see every day. This may alter people's' perception of you in ways that you are not even aware because you are not taking the time to look for these aspects of yourself that are flying under your own radar. Another factor in communication that people often miss is the importance of body language. The thoughts that you are thinking as well as the words that you are speaking do not always align very well with what your body is projecting. This can be problematic because often your body is communicating more about what is really going on than you are aware of. To catch essential details that your body language is indicating before others do you should always remain mindful of what you look like physically.

Eye contact is one crucial aspect of body language. Too little eye contact can give those who you talk to the impression that you are not very interested in what they are saying, while too much eye contact can make them feel intimidated or otherwise put off. The position of your arms can also communicate a lot. Crossed arms, for example, indicate standoffishness, while the direction of your arms when they are not crossed indicated where it is that you want to go or what you are interested in. You tend to point your chest and your feet at whatever it is that you are interested in, so be sure to look these at whoever you are speaking to when you talk.

The main message that you could take away from all of this is something along the lines of "to have a friend, be a friend." If you want to find success in your social life, you are going to have to put effort into relating to other people and helping them out. People are ultimately only out for themselves, for the most part, so to make your friends, you are going to need to give people whatever it is that you have to offer them. You should not, however, let yourself be taken advantage of. Give people as much as you determine they deserve from you, and you may get the same in return out of them.

# Chapter 8:
# The Effect of Genes on Habit Formation

All of our best and worst habits have foundations in psychological and neurobiological mechanisms. Habitual behaviors which are fixed in the brain for a certain amount of time, as well as more prospective and flexible ones, have a complex functioning and formation instead in one or multiple regions of the brain.

Of habits that are formed over a period of time, two main types should be gone over, stimulus-response (or SR) associations and more prospective and or cognitive processes. There is, however, another way of classifying these habit types that we can also use; by using the features of the neuronal activity associated with each and every habit.

Historically, habit formation has been looked at mainly through the lens of SR associations, which are usually picked up through continued habit reinforcement. These SR associations are typically made because there is simply little to no evidence indicating prospective or purposeful behavior. There is another process of learning by the name of the associated outcome (or AO). Learning these behaviors is due to a perceived reward for, usually, performing a specific task.

If, however, there happens to be a lousy reward involved in a particular task that is performed only due to specific SR associations, then a certain degree of insensitivity to the adversity associated with the task will usually be fostered. This is because the SR systems are strong enough to keep working even if the stimulus that they are after is either inadequate or ineffective. With all of this technical jargon set aside, it becomes clear here that it is easy to keep performing a task, possibly inadvertently, long after the perceived reward is still beneficial to you. This is yet another reason why any habits that are harmful to you should always be avoided in the first place; we are just not building with the mechanisms necessary to kick certain bad practices when they prove to be harmful.

SR and AO behaviors both have specific regions of the brain that they are most influenced and formed by. SR type behaviors (which function independently of perceived outcomes) are usually regulated in the following areas of the brain: the central amygdala nucleus, the infralimbic cortex, the substantia nigral compacta dopaminergic neurons, and the dorsolateral striatum. AO type behaviors (which always depend on perceived outcomes, as their name suggests) are usually caused within the associated cognitive circuits within the brain such as the dorsomedial striatum, the orbitofrontal cortex, and the prelimbic cortex.

One way to check how useful or purposeful a specific behavior happens to be is by observing the neuronal activity in the basal ganglia during the time at which the act is practiced. Throughout any sort of trial and error learning of a skill, habits are typically very much flexible and adjusted on the go. It is only later on when the habit has been sufficiently learned that it takes on a more static and solidly defined form. When you are learning how to perform a new task, it is always natural to go about whatever it is that you are doing rather slowly at first and then to work your way up towards performing the task with greater certainty and ease. There was once a study done on rats within a shaped maze which extols this happening well. When provided some type of reward for going a particular direction in the maze, the rats learned slowly and gradually to keep going in this direction and in this way, they eventually acquired whatever habit which would benefit them with the given reward. Their behaviors finally went from being sensitive to devaluation (or AO) to insensitive to it (or SR).

During these all-important periods of behavior acquisition, it is primarily the cortico-basal ganglia circuits of the brain that undergo the most significant amount of change in the activity of their neurons. Task responsive neurons often do the most firing in the periods in which tasks begin and complete. Throughout completing a particular task, these neurons are at their most inactive, especially when the work is one that is already established in the doer's brain. This gives someone performing a particular task an opportunity to relax a little and even multitask in some cases when he or she is performing an already mastered task.

Once a precise mechanism for performing a task has been created and cemented into the brain it is usually grouped together with specific other tasks of similar characteristics. This grouping together of these tasks makes neuronal connections quicker and more efficient among tasks of similar natures.

As far as the role of genes is concerned when analyzing the formation of new habits as well as the functioning of habits already established, their implications can be widely varied and not always certain. While individual genes can have profound influences on habits, there still remains lots of other factors that can have equally seminal effects on them, including psychosocial influences, external environment influences, and much, much more.

## Stephen Patterson

The most essential components of our anatomy, from the lens of a molecular genetic standpoint, are genes, molecules, information, DNA, and proteins, among other things. The role of proteins is to hold cells together, as well as form new hormones and neurotransmitters. Proteins are made out of amino acids, which initially have to be coded by DNA. These DNA chains have to be linked together to form new proteins within the organism.

There is a significant chain of creation that looks something like this: DNA, RNA, amino acids, proteins. It should also be noted that amino acids are hydrophobic, meaning that they stay away from water as much as possible. There are also enzymes, which are usually proteins of some sort and are responsible for catalyzing cellular reactions.

Mutations in genes would here be the main thing that would cause differences among people in habit formation. Of micro mutations there are three traditional types which go as follows: firstly, there are point mutations which entail some modification of just one letter in a genotype where the letter is only replaced by another letter. These point mutations typically do not have substantial impacts on the functioning of organisms because it is always just one letter being moved around. Then there are deletion mutations, in which one or more letters within a genotype are flatly deleted from it. These usually cause more detrimental effects on the organism than do point mutations. Finally, there are insertion mutations in which one or more letters are inserted into a genotype. Like deletion mutations, these insertion mutations typically have more significant impacts than point mutations on an organism. One somewhat surprising fact that should here be mentioned is that ⅔ of all modifications that ever happen do not lead to any real consequences.

95% of all DNA is noncoding, meaning that it does not have any effect on any RNA being produced. All of this DNA is then regulated by specific sequences, and it is only something called a transcription factor that can change a genotype before it has been translated into RNA or any further substance. These transcription factors are only found in the mitochondria of a cell. Since a sperm cell contains no mitochondria, there is, therefore, no mitochondrial DNA in which transcription factors can be found from the father passed on to his progeny. It is only from the mother that transcription factors can be passed down to offspring.

There are also slicing enzymes that, when mutated, create two entirely new proteins. This impact is only overshadowed by the effects of mutations in promoters and or transcription factors, which cause entire networks of new proteins within an organism. It is clear here that mutations in transcription factors have much more critical impacts on the functioning of an organism than do mutations in splicing enzymes.

Many different hormones and neurotransmitters have high impacts on the formation of habits as well as other things that should now be gone over. We will here start with some essential hormones:

Vasopressin controls social behaviors. Mutations in vasopressin receptors can cause significant changes in the social mechanisms of an organism.

Cortisol is a hormone that controls stress response. Excessive or deficient levels of cortisol can have adverse effects on your endocrine system.

Adrenaline is your body's fight or flight hormone. This tells us when to panic, which is helpful in the short term but can lead to health complications in the long run.

Serotonin can serve as your body's natural antidepressant and also causes the production of melatonin, which is your body's sleep hormone.

Dopamine is the pleasure hormone which regulates reward systems. This one is especially important in habit formation regarding classical pavlova conditioning, the basic premise of which goes something like "If I am rewarded with dopamine's, I repeat the action." Any stimulus-response habit is formed due in large part to this hormone.

Of neurotransmitters, the most important ones regarding habit formation are glucocorticoids. These control stress responses among other things, so mutations in glucocorticoid receptors will affect how an organism deals with stress.

One of the best and most reliable methods of determining what a genotype does for a particular organism is a method called cross-fostering. This method entails taking an organism at birth and putting it in a new environment with new parents. From here it would be necessary to consider both the genetic predispositions of the organism as well as the characteristics of the new environment and whatever parents are in the environment. Let's take a supposedly healthy child put into a situation with a schizophrenic stepmother for example. Since the child is in an environment with that disease entity, he or she becomes much more likely to develop schizophrenia his or herself. If the child was already born with a genetic predisposition to the disorder and was still placed in the environment with the schizophrenic, then the child's risk of developing the disorder will increase even more so. The same is valid for habit formation. If you are put into an environment in which everyone around you is messy, then you will be much more likely to become messy yourself. If we had to choose one or the other, it is probably the environment that has a more significant effect on habit formation than genes, though the two often work hand in hand. The age-old question of nature vs. nurture here boils down to one point: nurture develops on what nature allows.

The law of Brownian motion states that most molecules are subjected to random oscillations in motion which are influenced by external factors. This law applies to the heritability of traits passed on through the mitochondrial DNA of a mother to her offspring. Any chromosomes that feature one specific attribute are always going to be distributed randomly among any further divisions of the cell. This makes it more or less impossible to determine whether or not an offspring is ever going to develop a specific mutation or to determine how the DNA to RNA to the amino acid to protein transition is going to occur within the offspring.

Two of the most essential genes themselves that are responsible for changes in habit formation are NPY and MAO, both of which are responsible for anxiety reactions but mutations in the MAO gene can often cause increased degrees of aggression.

The role of genes regarding habit formation should never be given as much credence as that roles of environment and conscious decision making are. To focus on genes and or epigenetic change regarding habit formation rather than putting new habits into practice would be to hit all of the bullseyes on all of the wrong targets.

## Chapter 9:
## Stacking Habits

Habits are best used as little chains of performances stacked up one after the other. To stack these up most effectively, you first need to start implementing them daily. If you want to develop good habits, then it is easiest to group larger chains of individual habits together so that they can all be performed as one routine. This will ensure consistency in whatever it is that you are doing and will make performing many individual tasks much less overwhelming. The key to pulling this off, though, is persistence in the application of these tasks. These may seem like small things to observe at first, but their long-term implications accumulate over time to much loftier dimensions.

There are some steps involved in getting a habit to stick that should not be overlooked effectively. These include but are not limited to:

- Scheduling out a time for the activity;
- Identifying a trigger; and

- Planning out the steps required in performing this action.

Once you have set aside each and every component of a stack as an individual action, you must then create reminders for yourself to go through with all of these actions. If you do not do so, then you are bound to not follow through with many of your plans. Doing this can be overwhelming at first, but once you have developed these skills and others like them, you will be better able to perform all of these individual actions as an opaque whole in the future. This will improve your productivity dramatically.

If you want success in anything that you do, you are going to need to start off small. This includes mostly just building muscle memory for performing basic tasks at first. After you have completed some of these initial stages, you can then start moving on to other more complex matters. You will improve your consistency and performance over time— and eventually, the task, whatever it may be, will become more or less automatic for you.

We are now going to go over some of the most effective methods of building habits that will be beneficial to you in all of your endeavors.

### Start Out with Five-Minute Blocks.

## Stephen Patterson

The best way to ensure that you are going to follow through with a new habit every day is to make sure that the pattern is straightforward to practice. This can be done by environmental manipulation easily.

For example, if you wanted to get better at writing you, could start off small by only writing a paragraph a day. Doing this would cause forward momentum, which would, in turn, make the task much more natural to perform day in and day out as a sustained habit. You will eventually start to write more and more with each following day after a certain point.

This mini habit formation strategy can and should be applied to the stacks of habits that you put forth for yourself. In doing this, your initial stacks will not seem very large, but they will eventually grow as your individual habits increase. You do, however, have to remember to be consistent in these initial stages to get anywhere. Once you have built up some consistency, you can then start adding more and more habits to the stacks that you create.

One thing to keep in mind when forming new habits is time management. Once you have tried a habit for the first time, you can then determine just how much time it takes to complete the task. Try sticking to short time spans, five minutes for example, at first and then gradually work your way into performing the action for longer and longer lengths of time. A five-minute block of time to start out with may not seem to you like a long-time span, but even the shortest period of time spent on a task each day will invariably accumulate to equal a large number of hours over time.

**Look for Small Wins.**
Try to build your routines only around small habits that do not require a lot of effort to accomplish. Doing this will create lots of emotional momentum for you moving forward. If you keep this habit small and comfortable, at least at first, then this will aid you in remembering to perform them and will make habit formation much easier.

Small wins, in this case, could be defined as actions which do not require lots of willpower and are not very hard to perform. Examples of these could be taking vitamins each day, brushing your teeth, or writing a paragraph. If you start with these tasks which require little to no effort on your part, you will have more time and energy towards working on more difficult tasks. It is like Descartes' point on differentiating duties laid out in his Discourse on the method of rightly conducting the reason and seeking for truth in the sciences, you have to first focus on more manageable tasks and then move on to the more difficult tasks. It is a natural human tendency to focus on the hardest problems that we are beset with because they require the most attention, but what many people neglect to do when problem-solving is to break problems down into their smaller components and then piece together all of the steps necessary in solving the problem. If you want to avoid being overwhelmed by difficult tasks, then you need to focus on the easier tasks first.

To do this, you should track how much time it takes to complete specific tasks and then go about performing the duties that accompany the smallest amount of time before you get to anything else in a day.

**Pick A Location and A Time.**
It is much easier to stick to performing a task when you have already set aside a place and time for doing so. If you want to consistently complete the stacks of tasks that you set forth for yourself, then you are going to need to anchor them to specific times, locations, or combinations of both. Here are some examples of the prompts that you could set up for yourself to hold you accountable for performing your tasks.

In the morning you could set up a routine of things that you need to get done before you start your day. You could, for example, meditate, recite affirmations, and or read to start your day off on the right path. Some great ways to prompt yourself to perform these tasks every day would be to write these downs in your calendar and to keep the book you are reading next to your bed. Performing these actions each and every morning will have a very positive impact on the remainder of the day. Your mood, as well as your performance, will improve daily as a result of being persistent in these actions.

When you get to work in the morning, you could consider preparing yourself for more demanding tasks which the day is going to throw at you rather than just jumping right into all and any tasks that you need to complete. You could then start off on performing the smaller tasks that you need to complete and eventually work your way up into the larger tasks at hand. You could prompt yourself to take these steps by forbidding yourself to check your email before a certain hour, or by writing down the series of tasks that you need to complete for the day, ordered from easiest to hardest.

Next, we come to the middle of the day. This is when most people take as long at lunch as possible, so completing a stack of tasks at this time in the day will give you quite a competitive advantage in the long run. You should, however, expect to do this with little energy though, because you have just worked for 4 or so hours. This is why the tasks that you appropriate for this time need to be easier ones so that you can manage to do them with or without a lot of energy at your disposal.

After performing this stack, you should then take some time (not very much) to eat. And after you eat you should then go through any habits that will carry you through the rest of the day.

These habits could include going on a walk, meditating, or working out. One good way of motivating yourself to perform these tasks is to write them down in your calendar or to keep your walking shoes by your desk if your habit is to walk.

At the end of a workday, you should always make it a point to set yourself up for success for the following day. You can do so by performing another stack at the very end of the day. Doing this will make the next morning much easier for you, the only trick here is in reserving the energy throughout the day to perform this final set. Doing this will not only lighten the following day's workload, but it will also leave the workday on a positive note that will make you more eager to get to work the next day.

Prompts for doing this could be writing in a journal some tasks that you need to do the next day, or merely doing the tasks at hand if you find the time. Doing either one of these will increase your overall productivity in the long run.

**Anchor Your Stacks to Triggers.**
Triggers are, in this case, defined as motivators for performing specific tasks. These can take on all forms and are the only surefire way of reminding yourself to perform particular tasks.

Of triggers, there are two main types. These are as follows: External triggers, which are triggers put forth by things outside of you that create pavlova responses to them in your actions; and internal triggers, which are triggers that take place within your mind, such as emotions, thoughts, etc.

Anchoring your stacks of habits cannot only benefit you directly, but it can also help you indirectly since building stacks of good habits intentionally can prevent you from building stacks of negative ones unintentionally. These negative stacks can have detrimental impacts on your future, so it is important to be persistent in your observation and application of the decisive stacks.

While habit triggers can be extremely useful if you apply them correctly, they can also be harmful if misused or to meet the wrong ends. Take many of the social media sites up and running today for example. Most if not all of these sites study ways to apply triggers to get people to come back for more and more content every day. This can lead people into consuming much more social media than they really need and therefore wastes people's time.

The reason that some triggers become addictive while others never even catch on is that some offer greater rewards than others do. Without applying rewards to certain triggers, you cannot expect them to stick as much as they would otherwise.

If you use triggers consciously and to your advantage, then you will have a much easier time with establishing and maintaining positive habits rather than negative ones. Using this method will lead you to a much more successful habit formation.

When positive habits are stacked well, they become much easier to follow through with and usually a bit more efficiently performed. Grouping together all of the habits that go into executing a particular task will turn it into just another move that you have to follow through with—this will make it much easier for you to develop new skill sets and to increase your productivity.

**Successful Habits of Extraordinary People**

## Conclusion

Habit formation takes a long time to master so you cannot expect to get everything right just by reading one book and calling it quits. You need to, instead, keep expanding on your skills in doing this.

You should now start to apply the concepts laid out in this book to your everyday life. Make sure to be thorough when doing so if you want to reap the most significant rewards. Once you have started to apply the concepts to your everyday habits, you will begin to see results quicker than you might imagine.

It is always amazing the role that micro-habits have to play in the fostering of long-term success. People tend to wait around for magic beans when it comes to success rather than putting any hard and, more importantly, extended work into whatever it is that they are doing. They let their own judgments cloud their thinking with delusions surrounding their success. It is the multitude of small steps and habits that lead to success more so than large gestures and the bets made on chance happenings. The issue that most usually face is that they put all their faith in the latter and none in the former—this leads them to make little to no progress, though, because it is always the small things that accumulate to give you your successes in life.

Once you have finished applying each and every concept laid out in this book, you should then move on to gathering more ideas to apply to your habit formations from other sources. Doing this will help you continue to grow and expand on your skills.

**If you find this book helpful in anyway a review to support my endeavors is much appreciated.**

**Stephen Patterson**

## Successful Habits of Extraordinary People

www.ingramcontent.com/pod-product-compliance
Lightning Source LLC
Chambersburg PA
CBHW020400080526
44584CB00014B/1111